Canyonlands Needles District

Authored By Carolyn Rogalla

All national and international rights are reserved.

Copyright year 2018 by C. L. Rogalla

Published by CLR Southwest

11 Jun 2023

Unfortunately, our culture has evolved to filing law suits for any reason faulting the other person/company. Law suit filing is free, unless a lawyer is needed. Defending that law suit can destroy a person's life or company. Consequently, disclaimers are now a part of our society.

The five major books we've published have collectively over 460,000 words. Like the others, this book contains <u>massive amounts of exceptionally detailed information,</u> which we believe to be accurate, but there may be an error (s). If you find one, please email it so we can correct it immediately.

Note that we have <u>not hiked every</u> trail. For those not hiked, the data was gathered from text and/or talking with other hikers. We urge using of Internet to learn the latest status of those trails. Many trails and roads are not suitable for an average tourist – use caution and common sense. Carry a compass and/or GPS. IF GPS, *MARK* your parking lot and/or Trailhead location.

Always stop at each government (Park, BLM, etc.) visitor center to receive the most recent data on road and trail conditions. Knowing the weather conditions is vital as a canyon flash flood can kill you!

In summary,

> This book is a guide; **not an absolute fact.**

> **You are responsible** for your actions, not this book.

> When in doubt, use common sense.

> It was written as our hobby, not a profession.

> **If these terms are not acceptable, please do not purchase this book.**

The Needles

Five Faces

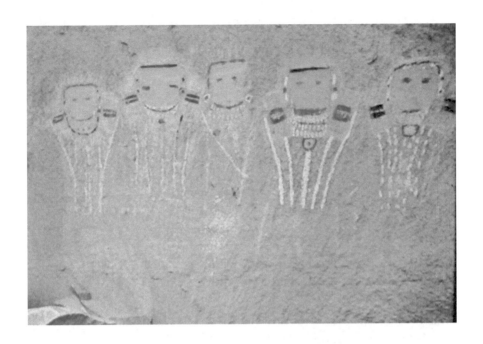

Village Ruin By Beef Basin

Disclaimer

Unfortunately, our culture has evolved to filing law suits for any reason faulting the other person/company. Law suit filing is free, unless a lawyer is needed. Defending that law suit can destroy a person's life or company. Consequently, disclaimers are now a part of our society. US has one lawyer per 300 people; China has one per 4,700 people. In US, it is a $160,000,000,000 business.

This book contains massive amounts of exceptionally detailed information, which we believe to be accurate, but there may be an error (s). If you find one, please email it so we can correct it immediately. Note that we have not hiked every trail. For those not hiked, the data was gathered from text and/or talking with other hikers. Many trails and roads are not suitable for an average tourist – use caution and common sense.

Carry a compass and/or GPS. IF GPS, *MARK* your parking lot and/or Trailhead location.

Always stop at each government (Park, BLM, etc.) visitor center to receive the most recent data on road and trail conditions. Knowing the weather conditions is vital as a canyon flash flood can kill you!

In summary:
This book is a guide; not an absolute fact.
You are responsible for your acts, not this book.
It was written as our hobby, not profession.
If these terms are not acceptable, please do not purchase this book.

****

Introduction to the Grand Circle Tour Books

Grand Circle is the name given to the major parks of Utah and the Grand Canyon that form a circle tour. These books visit the majority of those parks. They are also available in Kindle e-book format which are in color.

The purchase price of all these books is less than the cost of an average motel room for one night. A far greater value!

Book 1 -- Zion to Escalante, Utah:
Trip 1 **through** Trip 4, Tour 4-3
Parks covered are: Zion, Kolob Canyon, Cedar Breaks, Bryce Canyon, Kodachrome State Park, Grand Staircase-Escalante and Calf Creek.
Note: E-Book is the only one that has Mormon History.

Book 2 – Escalante, to Moab Utah:
Trip 4, Tour 4-4, **through** all of Trip 6.
Parks covered are: Goblin Valley, San Rafael Swell, Capitol Reef, Canyonlands - Maze District, Arches National Park and Canyonlands Island in the Sky.
Note: The print book has less content that the e-book due to page restrictions.

Book 3 - Vermilion Cliffs and North Rim Grand Canyon Guide
Grand Canyon, Kaibab National Forest (west Grand Canyon area), The Wave, geological chaotic White Pocket, Buckskin Gulch, Pink Sand Dunes, Lees Ferry, Colorado River and, Wupatki Indian Ruins.

Book 4 - Moab, Utah to Monument Valley.
Canyonlands Needles District Newspaper Rock displaying ancient Indian petroglyphs, Monument Valley, Natural Bridges National Monument, Hovenweep ancient Anasazi Ruins National Monument, Navajo National Monument and Gooseneck State Park. Included are many extraordinary scenic canyon hikes to ancient Anasazi Indian ruins.

Book 5 Title: Needles – Canyonlands. Printed in full color. - This is **book** focuses on Canyonlands-Needles District only. Data is also contained in print Book 4 which is black and white only.

Book 6 *Canyon de Chelly to Grand Canyon* (continuing to Cameron, Az.). Parks and landmarks covered are: Canyon De Chelly, Hubbell Trading Post, Petrified Forest and the Painted Desert, Homol'ovi Indian Ruins State Park, Rock Art Ranch Petroglyphs, Meteor Crater, Historic Two Guns Area, Historic Diablo Canyon Bridge, Turkey Tanks and Grand Falls, Walnut Indian Canyon, Historic Route 66, Oatman, South Rim Grand Canyon, and Chloride's Purcell Painted Murals.

Note: The North Rim Grand Canyon is extensively covered in Book 3, *Vermilion Cliffs and North Rim Grand Canyon Guide*

Book 7 –. The Wave, Cottonwood Cove, White Pockets and Coyote Buttes Its content is also included in Book 3, *Vermilion Cliffs and North Rim Grand Canyon*, in black and white photographs. This abbreviated book is in full color. Color is mandatory to truly appreciate the magnificence of its chaotic geology further enhanced by its colors.

Internet site to order all books is:
http://www.southutahparks.com/

****

Book Tour Content

This book is a combination of driving, walking, Mountain Biking and other tours such as horseback riding. There are suggestions of what to see and do, for each tour.

A well-planned vacation/holiday ensures pleasant memories so that no day is wasted. This book incorporates approximately 10 web sites, 11 video sites of roads and trails, 76 photographs, 85 GPS and 13 maps. We also identify free dry-camp (no facilities) sites to reduce travel expenses.

Mile-By-Mile and GPS Location

When driving, your exact location is accomplished by using a meticulous identification of mileposts (posts along the road indicating mileage) located at each mile (1.6 km) on every improved road. Where those mileposts are not available, we use actual miles from a designated reference point.

Where applicable, Global Positioning Satellite data (GPS) is supplied to complement walking adventures in remote areas. Using this collection of information, you will always know your exact location.

Book Navigation

Book organization starts with the *Table of Contents*. Under each of the major trips, there are *individual Tours*. In that individual Tour, data is organized into the following segments:

1.0 *Information*; 2.0 *Visitor Center*; 3.0 *Services*; 4.0 *Lodging*; 5.0 *Camping*, 6.0 *Hiking*; 7.0 *Other Tours* (Biking, Horse, etc.) and 8.0 *Driving Tours*. E-books have many hyperlinks to leap from one section any other.

Summary

We are sure this book will make your vacation more memorable and successful. If you consider this book to be helpful to others, **please submit a book review** where you purchased this book.

Table of Contents.

Number at end of each line is the page number.

To Canyonlands, Needles District 9

>> **A Alternate Route From Monticello 9**

>> **B Road to Needles on Road 211 from Highway 191 9**

>> **C Park Road into Needles Park 17**

>> **D Canyonlands - Needles District 19**

>>> **Driving on Sand Road Instructions 52**

---------**4-Wheel Vehicle for Sand ---------- 53**

---------**Fat Tire Bicycles for Sand---------- 53**

Tour 1-03-01 - Colorado River Overlook 53

Tour 1-03-02 - Elephant Hill Road 56

  Devils Lane Junction 59

Tour 1-03-03 – To Horse Canyon via Cave Spring and Salt Creek 64

Tour 1-03-04 - Route To Horse Canyon 65

Tour 1-03-05 - Beef Basin & Bobby's Hole 73

Tour 1-03-06 - Davis and Lavender Canyons 81

  To Davis Canyon 83

  To Lavender Canyon 86

Appendix 1 - Dugout Ranch History 89

Appendix 2 Desert Hiking Medical Problems 91

To Canyonlands, Needles District

The applicable map is the 1982 U.S. Geological *La Sal* 1:100,000. The route to the Needles District is very scenic. **Needles Outpost** is a small tourist friendly commercial campground with hot showers, a mini-market, tour books and friendly information.

The tour starts with typical desert mesas, hills and then narrows as it enters a canyon just before **Newspaper Rock** that is adjacent to fast flowing Indian Creek, if there is no drought. After a few miles, the narrow canyon widens into a historic farm and ranching valley, bordered by towering red cliffs.

>> A Alternate Route From Monticello

Northbound tourists going to Canyonlands-Needles can save considerable time by driving on Blue Mountain/Harts Draw Loop Road 136 that joins Highway 211 at MP 9.8. The only disadvantage is the gradual elevation change from 7,046-feet (2,148 m) to 8,863-feet (2,701 m) and many turns.

M 00 At the Visitor Center (200 S). Driving west.
M 05.0 Dalton Springs **Campground** to left.
M 06.5 Buckboard **Campground** to left.
M 18.8 Junction with Highway 211 at MP 8.7. Turn left.

>> B Road to Needles on Road 211 from Highway 191

The road to Needles has three segments:
1) State of Utah Highway 211,
2) Bureau of Land Management (BLM) and the
3) National Park Service. Using mileposts, which are infrequent, becomes confusing; therefore, the prime source will be actual miles.

M 0.0 Starting at milepost 19.4 (Road 211), from Highway 191 at MP 86.1. There is an information Kiosk at this junction.
M 0.2 Abandoned oil well to the right
M 2.5 Occasionally, local native Indians are selling Indian jewelry. See Appendix 3.
M 3.2 The old farm houses north was the **Home of Truth** - a religious group established by Marie Snyder Ogden.

Her house is in the back with a large wooden porch. Buildings were crudely constructed by the members. Most have no insulation other than cardboard and newspapers. Water was obtained from a windmill-driven pump that filled a few concrete tanks. The soil and weather did not favor farming.

Marie was born on 31 May 1883 in Newark, New Jersey. She married Harry Ogden, a successful insurance executive, and had one daughter, Roberta. Harry died in 1929 at which time Marie turned to religion for solace. As a widow, she devoted her energies to the socialite circles where she eventually became the president of the Women's Federation Club.

She traveled west as far as Boise, Idaho, preaching that the earth would be in turmoil and governments would topple. She believed, at that time, the devil would rise to earth and declare himself as the ruler. Then Jesus would appear at this location to dispel the devil and become the final ruler. Therefore, this land was sacred. Those who believed would be protected by a halo of light through this turmoil.

Marie, with 30 followers from New Jersey, Idaho and Chicago left their homes and arrived here in 1933. The commune may have grown to one hundred. Like all religious cult members, they gave their material goods to Marie to create a communal cooperative with divisions of work and sharing of possessions. They promised to follow her teachings, without question. She believed in:

1. Reincarnation and resurrection,
2. Conversations with the dead,
3. She was the reincarnation of the Virgin Mary (mother of Jesus).

Marie continued to have revelations from God. Once settled, they started to publish pamphlets and spread them around the area.

She purchased the San Juan Record newspaper in 1934 and used that media to promote her religion. In 1935 it was learned that Mrs. Ogden housed the deceased body of Mrs. Edith Pesha that she was preserving by washing her with salt three times daily and forcing food into her daily. Mrs. Odgen was convinced she could restore her soul and bring her back to life. Soon the local sheriff, district attorney and the state board of health learned of this event. Since the body was "preserved" and no laws violated, no legal action could be taken. Eventually, Mrs. Odgen abandoned her goal and the body was cremated.

The group dwindled to about seven followers. All the possessions were auctioned in September of 1977 by the last member of the group. He destroyed all documents to preserve a positive image of the commune. Unfortunately, that also destroyed the history of the group.

Mrs. Odgen left the compound and taught music until the late 1960s when she died in a Blanding nursing home on 4 March 1975 at the age of 91years, ending another phase of history in this valley. The Monticello Museum has a small display of this era. Today, some of the restored buildings are used for Art Shows and small festivals.

M 9.8 Junction with *Blue Mountain/Harts Draw Loop Road 136.*
M 10.1 – 11.6 Steep downhill road.

Indian Creek Unit
Bear Ears National Monument

An area of 1,351,849 acres (547,074 ha.) was declared a National Monument by President Obama on 28 December 2016, three weeks before leaving office. It covered a massive area from Goosenecks State Park (Tour 2-08) to the south and Anticline Overlook (Tour 1-01) to the north.

Due to various national political and Utah State events, the 2016 Bears Ears National monument was reconfigured in December of 2017 by President Trump. Its area was reduced from 1.35 million acres (546,329 ha.) to 201,876 acres (81,696) resulting in two separate geographical units. This is eastern border of the Indian Creek Unit as shown in the map below encompassing 71,876 acres (29,095 ha.). The western border is Needles Park. The Monticello BLM and USFS have prime management responsibility augmented by a coalition of five Indian tribes.

As seen from almost anywhere in this area, Bear Mountain profile resembles the ears of a bear created by two buttes. One ear is at 8,930-foot (2,717 m) elevation while the other is at 9,058 feet (2,756 m).

It is known to several native Indian Tribes as: *Hoon'Naqvut, Shash Jáa, Kwiyagatu Nukavachi* and *Ansh An Lashokdiwe* or just Bear Ears. Of course, it is sacred and woven into their oral history.

This is one of many, many *Changing Woman* legends among various local Indian tribes. A sign at Natural Bridges touring loop informs us:

*One of the more popular Navajo stories is that of Changing-Bear-Maiden, who was very beautiful and desired by many men. She would have nothing to do with them. However, Coyote * (Áltsé hashké), the trickster, persuaded Changing-Bear Maiden to marry him in spite of her brothers' warning that the union would bring evil.*

She began to change and by winter's end her transformation into a mischievous bear was complete. Realizing that the only way to save her was to change her into another form, her brothers killed Changing-Bear-Maiden, cutting off her ears and threw them away. They became the buttes seen today.

* A coyote that looks like a coyote in <u>animal image</u>, but looks like a man with a mustache in <u>human image</u>.

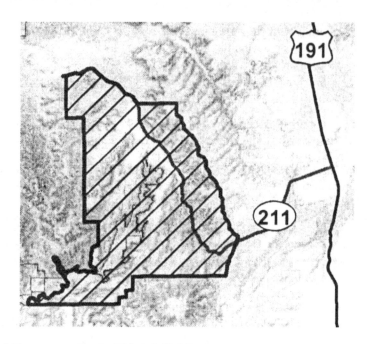

M 12.5 **Newspaper Rock**. This is MP 6.7.

Parking lot is adequate for any sized RV. There is a chemical toilet in the parking lot. These are the best petroglyphs on this tour, recording about 900 years of Indian occupation, displaying over 300 images. The oldest figures appear to be the art at the top of the rock. Images of horses indicate these were made after 1540 A.D. when the Spanish introduced the horse into Southwest America. Bear paws are the symbol of the Hopi Indian Bear Clan. Look to the upper right where there are four bear paw prints. One large and three smaller. Three of those have six toes – should be five toes.

When the ancient people (Anasazi/Hopi) emerged from the underground to earth's surface, individual groups of people assigned clan names to themselves. The Bear Clan being the first, Strap the second and Bluebird Clan the Third. Therefore, a bird-head image could be the symbol of that clan.

Please do not touch any of these petroglyphs as human oil and salt tends to destroy them.

M 13.0 (MP 6.1) At ground level, visible from the road to the right, are petroglyphs of abstract design having a bird head, sheep and other figures. Notice the bird-head image.

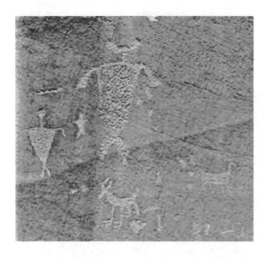

M 15.5 Entering a large valley with many Cottonwood trees.

M 16.3 Former **Harry Green Ranch** is located to the distant left where only a red chimney remains. This Texan was mayor of Moab in 1903 and influential in establishing Moab's first bank about seven-years later. The ranch itself probably existed in the 1880s. It was owned by Harry around the early 1900s. In 1927, it was purchased by S & S Ranch (Dugout Ranch history – Appendix 1).

M 16.7 **Rock Climbing Cliffs** - Huge parking lot for rock climbers who climb these tall vertical cliffs. They favor routes where there is a vertical crack to use as a hand hold. There is a chemical toilet.

M 17.9 **Titus Ranch** - Originally from Illinois, Joseph Titus married in Monticello in 1894. He and his wife moved to this area in 1899 and started this ranch. S & S purchased the ranch in 1918 and Joe became their foreman.

M 18.6 **Joe Donnelley Ranch** - Only a red rock chimney remains of this ranch. Around 1910, it was owned by Joseph Davis, for whom Davis Canyon may have been named. The next year, it was purchased by Donnelley who sold to it Al Scorup in late 1921.

M 19.3 <u>**End of Highway 211 and Start of BLM road**</u>

M 19.7 **Dugout Ranch** - To the left are a series of ranch houses that are the historic Dugout Ranch. See the history of this ranch in Appendix 1. The land is now owned by Canyon Land Research Center; however, the family still has cattle ranching rights. The reservoir to the right stores water from Indian Creek for this cattle ranch.

M 20.5 Paved/gravel road to **Beef Basin and Bobby's Hole** to the left. There is a chemical toilet and large parking area where camping may be allowed. Confirm at the kiosk that also has a map. On the opposite side of the bulletin board is a place to post your personal message. See Tour 1-03-05.

M 26.3 **Superbowl Campground.** This multi-loop campground provides 37 campsites, with each site having a tent/trailer space, a picnic table, a fire ring, and vault toilets. There is no water at the campground. Campsites are first-come, first-served and self-register at the campground. The camping fee is $15 per site/per night. At the end, small area that can accommodate about 3-4 large RV's.

M 26.7 **Road to Davis and Lavender Canyon**. Against the distant cliffs was a potential site for dumping nuclear waste. See Tour 1-03-06.

M 27.6 **Creek Pasture Campground**.

The large one-loop campground provides 32 campsites that each feature a tent/trailer space, a picnic table, a fire ring, and vault toilets. Each campsite can hold 10 people and 2 vehicles. There is no water at the campground. Campsites are $15 per night and are "first come, first served" and self-register at the site. The *Creek Pasture Group Site* may be reserved in advance on the Internet.

North and South Six Shooter Buttes. For our foreign friends, six-shooter is another name for a revolver (pistol) that has six bullets in its cylinder. The buttes silhouette resembles the barrel of that revolver.

M 29.6 **Indian Creek Falls BLM Campground.** This is Lockhart Road 122 named after L. B. Lockhart. At mile 0.5, 0.6 and 0.8, there are single open primitive camp sites to the left.

At *M 1.0* **Hamburger Rock Campground** has about ten sites, plus a couple of remote sites. It favors tents and small RV camping around a large flat rock with one chemical toilet. Few sites are shaded by juniper trees; otherwise the huge rock provides shade. Campsites are $15 per night and available on a first come, first served basis. Each site features a tent/trailer space, a picnic table, a fire ring, and vault toilets. There is no water at the campground.

At *M 3.0* is **Indian Creek Falls** Group site. Reservations are required only for the group site that has a chemical toilet. It has tent/trailer space, picnic tables, a fire ring, and a vault toilet and space for about 10 vehicles, with a vehicle and trailer counting as two vehicles. There is no water. Reservation information at (435) 587-1500

M 3 – 5 Along these last two miles (3.2 km), narrow roads branch off the main road to some flat areas for camping. Overall, approximately 15 camping areas can be found. After about another mile, the road drops down to Indian Creek. If water is flowing, there is a 15-20-foot (4.6 to 6 m) water fall with a swimming pool at the bottom. This is where the 1859 Macomb Expedition camped in Tour 1-01 at M 7.3. The road further requires a high clearance 4-Wheel drive road to Moab, not covered in this tour book.

M 32.3 **Entering Canyonlands National Park**

Crossing over a cattleguard and entering the Needles Park boundary which was a crude dirt road until 1967, when it was enlarged to a two-lane road.

Needles Outpost Visitor

M 33.8 Turn right for 0.7-miles.

When Needles became a National Park, Dick Smith imagined a resort here that included a swimming pool in a natural sandstone rock depression. He was a local airplane pilot who was born in this area and simply loved it.

Originally, this was Utah state property, available for a 99-year lease, which Dick obtained in 1965. Selling stock at $5,000 per share, he built a small cafe, gasoline station, shower house and an airplane landing strip. Electricity was provided by diesel generators. Water was brought in by truck from a well located within the park because his well-drilling failed. He used his airplane to take tourists across Canyonlands. In 1973, he crashed his airplane while trying to find bighorn sheep for the Park and a wildlife organization. All people aboard died. His family assumed operation of this resort and sold it to his friend and pilot Jay Pratt.

In 1979, a mystery midnight fire burned down the main building. The resort became inactive until 1984 when Mark and Chris Davis purchased all resort rights. They rebuilt the Visitor Center on the same foundation, refurbished the showers and added sewer and water facilities for RVs (no longer active). Water was piped to tent camp sites (water no longer supplied). They also replaced electric generators. They renamed it as Needles Outpost and it was successful.

It had a couple different owners until May 2017 when Nature Conservatory purchased it to preserve it from any future development.

It remains a full-service tourist friendly facility, offering a campground, minimarket, firewood, gasoline (no diesel), propane, ice, soft drinks, books and a small airport. Showers and flush toilets are in a separate building. They sell disposable waste bags and portable toilets, if available. They have a huge solar energy panel.

Campground - This is a family type of campground having designated quiet hours. If no one is at the store to register, just drive in and pay the following day. All sites have a picnic table and a fire pit. Campground reservations are available at their Internet site. Rental of camping tents, sleeping bags is offered.

The store/office is open from 9:00 AM to 6:00 PM from 15 February to 1 December. Confirm dates at their Internet site as weather determines the exact dates.

Their cell phone number is (435) 459 0777. Internet: **http://www.needlesoutpost.com/**

Everyone is welcome to their services for a small fee. However, this is <u>not a free repository</u> for your BLM garbage. Showers require a special token that can be purchased at the store.

IF you use their dump station, **Do NOT** use bleach or formaldehyde chemicals in your RV tanks (or any time) because it will destroy the bacteria in their septic tank, requiring <u>very expensive restoration</u>.

Note: They have an air compressor to refill your tires if you deflated them for sand driving.

M 34.6 **Ranger booth** to pay an entry fee.

Canyonlands-Needles Visitor Center

M 35.0 Visitor Center to the right.

Note: **Colorado Overlook Road** is north of the Visitor Center. See Tour 1-0301.

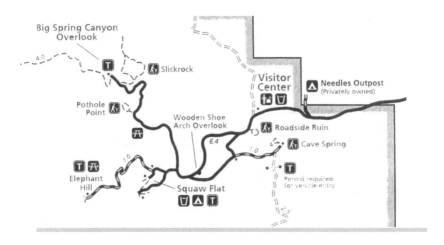

>> C Park Road into Needles Park

Leaving Visitor Center

M 35.4 **Roadside Ruins** is a 300-yard walk to an unusually preserved granary storage house tucked under a low ledge. It is considered to be of Anasazi origin, probably from the Mesa Verde, Colorado culture expansion to this area.

Interestingly, this ruin is almost covered with original dirt/mud mortar with very little exposed rock. Do not climb on the ledge or anyway disturb this precious ruin so that others may enjoy it.

The Fremont Indian's art was also in this area, but they left no ruins. Typical of the Anasazi, beans, squash and corn were the principle crops augmented by berries. Local wild animals supplied the meat. As with other areas of Utah, the Anasazi abandoned their villages in the early 1300s for reasons unknown, but it was thought to be from extended drought.

M 35.6 **Loop Salt Creek Road** and Ranger residence to the left. This 2-mile (3.2 km) loop road exits at M 37.5 below. It is the access road to Salt Creek and Horse Canyon 4-Wheel Drive roads. It also passes *Wooden Shoe* group camping site.

M 37.1 **Wooden Shoe Arch** - This unique arch resembles a shoe. It is best photographed about 2 hours before sunset with 200 mm lens.

M 37. 5 Loop road to Salt Creek.

M 37.8 Junction. Road to Squaw Flat Campgrounds and Big Spring. Turn left to the campgrounds.

M 38.1 Junction to Campground 'B' and Elephant Hill. Turn right.

<u>End of Driving Tour from Highway 191</u>

****

To Big Spring and Pothole Point

Note: The parking lot fills quickly during spring/fall season.

M 0.0 From M 37.8 above, continuing to Big Spring.

M 1.7 Three shaded **picnic tables**.

M 2.1 **Pothole Point**. There is a trail leading to the top of the butte where there are many small potholes in the rock that store water.

M 3.4 **Slickrock Foot Trail.** This is a very popular and easy short loop trail described in Paragraph 6.0 - Hiking.

M 3.7 **Big Spring**. Road ends at a large parking lot. The mushroom shaped boulders and the valley below provide a serene scenic view at sunset or sunrise.

The principal trailhead is Confluence Trail that goes to an overlook where the Colorado and Green Rivers merge, forming the classic Colorado River. See Paragraph 6.0 – Hiking, for details. It is illegal to feed wild animals.

* *

>> D Canyonlands - Needles District

1.0 Introduction

Needles consists of 337,570-acres (136,610 ha.) having an elevation span from 3,700-feet (1,128 m) to 7,000-feet (2,134 m). Its size overwhelms all other Utah parks. For example, it is 10 times the size of Bryce. It hosts over 100-miles (160 km) of established trails, 30-miles (48 km) of paved roads and 40 (64 km) of 4-Wheel Drive (4-WD) roads that require vehicles have a dual range transmission. The most evil is 4-WD road Elephant Hill Road. The Park was created by President Johnson September 1964.

This park's attractive feature is a lack of people because most of Needles scenery is in the backcountry. Unlike other parks in our tours, there are adventures beyond its borders offering unlimited primitive hiking opportunities at Beef Basin in Tour 1-03-05. That is, not on well-defined trails. Rosalia de Castro best described these remote hiking opportunities when she wrote: *I see my path, but I do not know where it leads. Not knowing is what inspires me to travel it.*

Because of varied, confusing and intertwining trails; it is impossible to precisely describe the trails and their junctions. This can only be done with a trail map shown in Paragraph 6.0 – Hiking.

In the summer, canyon temperatures can exceed 100-degrees F (38 C), which evaporates scarce spring water, necessitating that you carry water. See Appendix 1. Trails meander up and down canyons, increasing travel times; however, the elevation changes are minor, except for Lower Red Lake.

The best map is *National Geographic Trails Illustrated No. 210* for Canyonlands that can be purchased from local bookstores or the park Visitor Center. A more detailed map is the *La Sal* 1:100,000 scale map.

In the summer, canyon temperatures can exceed 100-degrees F (38 C), which evaporates scarce spring water, necessitating that you carry water. Read and understand Appendix 2. Introductory video of Needles:
https://www.youtube.com/watch?v=RmyHp6Gbn1g

What to See/Do

Chesler Park is the primary attraction of this park, favoring an overnight hike to explore the entire area.

Next is a multi-day hike through Salt Creek, where ancient Anasazi ruins decorate isolated Salt Creek Canyon. At the center of that trail is the remarkable pictograph of the ***All-American Man.*** There are many petroglyphs and pictographs along the trail.

> Petroglyphs: These images are 'pecked' into a flat rock surface.

> Pictograph: These images are painted onto a flat rock surface.

Rules: Do not touch or breathe on these images as the salt/oil on your skin deteriorates them. Absolutely do NOT add any graffiti! Watch your children! Do not enter or climb on or touch any ruin. Do not take any artifacts, broken pottery, etc. Leave them for others to appreciate.

Law: There are many federal laws protecting Indian artifacts. Prison sentences can be up to ten years, plus huge fines.

There are several **4-Wheel driving tours**. If you are experienced with 4-Wheel driving, a drive on Elephant Hill is a major adventure that leads to many trailheads, saving miles of walking. Elephant Hill is considered one of the most difficult 4Wheel drive roads in Utah, especially the back-side (return route)! Long wheel base vehicles should not attempt this journey.

An easy 4-Wheel drive trip is to **Confluence Overlook** from the Visitor Center. This is where the Green River merges with the Colorado River, making it the mighty Colorado River that carved the canyons, most notably the Grand Canyon.

4-Wheel Vehicle Rental

Many rental companies at Moab, Utah – Internet search: *moab 4 wheel rental*

Historic Cowboy Camps

There are four such campgrounds used by cowboys since the 1910s until the area became a National Park:

1) Cave Spring Trail.
2) Lost Canyon Cowboy Camp.
3) Devil's Lane at SOB.
4) Between campgrounds CP4 and CP5.

Restrictions

1. No pets are allowed in backcountry areas or on trails. At all other places they must be on a 6-foot leash.

2. No **ATVs, UTVs or OHVs** are allowed anywhere, including RZRs.

3. Mountain bikes are allowed only on roads.
4. A permit is required to camp in the backcountry.
5. Water is scarce. Conserve every drop
6. Fires allowed at designated camping sites; otherwise, use a portable stove.
7. All vehicles must be state licensed, including motorcycles that must be street legal. Drivers of those vehicles must also be licensed. You must stay on designated roads--no off-road traveling.
8. Special Bear proof containers are required at all areas of Salt Creek hike, and depending on distant mountain food supply, they may migrate to Lost Canyon.
9. Disposable human waste bags are required for overnight back country hiking

Climate

The average climate data below is not precise due to desert/mountains conditions that change rapidly. Therefore, a general guide.

Temperatures at canyon bottoms are at least 10% higher and very arid (low humidity). Late summer months are prone to very heavy rains that cause canyon flash floods that can kill you if you camp at the bottom. Winter snow makes back road impassable especially to Beef Basin.

Average English Units (F & Inches)

	Jan	Feb	Mar	Apr	May	Jun
Temp	44/22	52/28	64/35	71.42	82/51	93/60
Precip	1.81	1.3	1.18	0.94	1.02	0.63
	Jul	Aug	Sep	Oct	Nov	Dec
Temp	100/67	97/66	88/55	74/42	56/30	45/23
Precip	1.34	1.85	1.54	1.89	1.42	1.26

Precip. = Precipitation (rain and snow)

Average Metric Units (C and Cm)

	Jan	Feb	Mar	Apr	May	Jun
Temp	5.6/-5.6	11/-2.2	18/1.7	22/5.6	28/11	34/16
Precip.	4.6	3.3	3	2.4	2.6	1.6
	Jul	Aug	Sep	Oct	Nov	Dec
Temp	38/19	36/19	31/13	23/5.6	13/-1.1	7.2/-5
Precip.	3.4	4.7	3.6	4.8	3.6	3.2

Geology

Cedar Mesa Sandstone geology is the soul of this park making it the most attractive of all three Canyonlands Parks. These formations are also found in Canyonlands-Maze District. All formations are from the Pennsylvanian and Permian times (245 to 330 million years ago) and again during Triassic and Jurassic times (144 to 245 million years ago). The oldest of these formations are near the Green and Colorado confluence.

Recall that the western barrier was the Sierra Nevada Mountains in California. That mountain range started to form only four million years ago.

Consequently, during the Pennsylvania period, sea water flowed into the area and eventually evaporated. This Pennsylvania period cycle repeated itself forming a sedimentary layer 3,000-feet (94 m) thick. Those layers were later covered by mud and sandstone. During the Permian time, sand dunes and loose soil/sediments were deposited by periodic floods from the Uncompahgre Mountains that contained iron saturated sediments. Only 1 to 3% of iron in the sand deposits is necessary to create red and pink colors. This formation became the pink and white layers of **Cedar Mesa Sandstone** seen at Needles. The Uncompahgre Plateau is located in western Colorado created by the Colorado Plateau uplift.

The Triassic period was one of rivers and streams depositing mud and sand that are now the Moenkipi and colorful Chinle formations. The Jurassic era brought huge sand dunes that evolved to the Wingate and Navajo Sandstone formations that became the cliffs we see today. These sands were solidified into rock by silica, calcium carbonate or iron oxide. The latter ($CaCO_3$) also form the very dense rock calcite.

All formations are subject to water, wind and chemical erosion. Chemical erosion is caused by carbonic acid that is a standard product of organic decay. When the acids dissolve the hard stone, the wind and water (especially ice) attack the weaker rock. As a narrow cliff fin is being dissolved, a hole is formed at which time wind and water forces become dominate. As the hole enlarges, larger blocks of sandstone fall eventually creating an arch. An arch, as opposed to a square structure, is durable as witnessed in many architectural designs from Roman aqueducts to massive European churches.

The three geological divisions of Needles are listed below.

1) Western part has Grabens as described in the Elephant Road tour at Devils Lane;

2) Central, which incorporates Chesler Park forming narrow vertical fins. Here, pressure from underground formations upward caused the surface to crack. Like Arches National Park, once cracked, erosion started to form the spires.

3) Eastern segment primarily composed of cliffs with corresponding canyons.

2.0 Visitor Center

General park information, including hiking and camping permit information.
https://www.nps.gov/cany/planyourvisit/needles.htm

There are two Visitor Centers providing slightly different services:

1. Privately owned **Needles Outpost Visitor Center** - Needles Outpost was described earlier as we entered this park.

2. **Government owned Needles Park Visitor Center** is the official Visitor Center. It is open 8 AM to 5 PM from April to late October but closes for the winter. **Note:** While the Visitor Center is closed, the park remains open all year. If hiking, register at the trailhead. Unfortunately, the gate to Horse Canyon is closed since ice covers the water holes that may break. Also, there is no towing service in the winter.

Free water is available at this center when open.

The center has a book store, small museum and an auditorium that shows a 15-minute video on the entire Canyonlands Park (not specific to Needles). Backcountry and camping permits can be purchased here. We highly recommend reading their backcountry road and hiking notebooks to fully understand backcountry hiking trails and driving roads. Topographic maps can be purchased for backpacking into the remote areas. See Paragraph 6.0, Hiking for topographic map description.

Phone numbers: There is no cell phone coverage.
  -Emergency 911
  -Visitor Center: (435) 259-4711.
-Camping and Hiking reservations: (435) 259-4351
Monday – Friday from 8AM to 12PM, Mountain Time.
  -Road conditions:
  https://www.nps.gov/cany/planyourvisit/road-conditions.htm

3.0 Services - None

4.0 Lodging - None

5.0 Camping

BLM and National Forest camping is allowed anywhere outside the Canyonlands National Park borders, except on private land at Dugout Ranch, where fences establish those borders. There are three BLM improved sites that were identified on the road into Needles Park in Tour 1-03 >>B at M 26.3, 27.8 and 29.6.

Needles National Park

Needles Park Internet **reservation** sites:

1. Elephant Hill Road- Improved campgrounds: **https://canypermits.nps.gov/**

2. In-park camping: **https://www.recreation.gov/** In the search bar, type in: *Canyonlands National Park Needles District Campground*

   At the new page, click on the subject above. Select Camping *Loop A*.
   Phone: (877) 444-6777 or +1 518-885-3639 (International).

3. Needles overnight backcountry: **https://canypermits.nps.gov/**
Phone: (435) 259-4351.

   Note: A camping permit includes a backcountry hiking permit.

Disposable Human Waste Bags

These are required for overnight camping at:
  1) Peekaboo and New Bates Wilson vehicle campground.
  2) Backcountry hiking campsites.
  3) Within 1/2 mile of the Green and Colorado Rivers.
All group camping sites must bring their own toilet, or equivalent.

Typical waste bag brands are PETT, BIFFY, WAG or Rest Stop II. There are YouTube videos of each product. Suggest viewing the BIFFY first. The Visitor Center sells the Rest Stop II (subject to change). Return all used disposable bags to the Visitor Center for disposal.

Needles Park Campground

Squaw Flat is the official Needles Park Campground, having a total of 26 sites. Maximum RV length is 28 feet (8.6 m). There are no RV facilities. Fire grates and picnic tables are available at each site. Flush toilets with water are available at each campground. Camp water is available spring through fall seasons at selected areas in the campground.

There are two general camping sections: A and B. Each site is limited to 10 people and 2 vehicles per site. Campground A is on the east side of a large butte, enjoying the warm sunrise. It is open all year. Campground A's fourteen sites may be reserved from 15 March through 30 June and 1 September through 31 October, six months in advance of arrival. Otherwise, it is First-come/First-served.

Campground A has the amphitheater for Ranger talks.

Campground B is 800 yards further on the west side, enjoying sunsets. All 13 sites are First-come/First-served. It may close during winter months based on demand. Each site has a tag with an expiration date. Suggest talking to those people whose occupancy will end soon and arrange for a transfer time.

Group Sites

There are three group sites that may be reserved from mid-March to mid-September, six months prior to arrival.

1. **Wooden Shoe**, located on Salt Creek/Ranger Loop Road. Maximum 25 people/5 vehicles.
2. **Squaw Flat** "A" Camp Site. Maximum 50 people/10 vehicles.
3. **Split Top** Group Site, located on road to Salt Creek. Maximum 15 people/3 vehicles.

Backcountry Camping Permits

General backcountry information is found at:
https://www.nps.gov/cany/planyourvisit/backcountry.htm

Allocation is by *Zone* and *Site*. The zones are: Needles North (northern), Red Lake/Grabens (western), Butler/West Side Canyons (south), Salt/Horse (east-northeast) and Davis/Lavender (east-southeast).

These are identified by a green color border on the Park trail map. They are also identified on the National Geographic Trails Illustrated (TI) Map *Canyonlands National Park Needles & Island In The Sky* - 210 (ISBN 0-925873-10-1). TI map covers Needles, Island in the Sky and the far-east section of the Maze.

Applying for a Permit

Once your request is received, and money paid, your permit will be sent by email. Please print your permit and have it with you during your trip. If you are not able to print your permit, you must have either a digital copy or your permit number available. Click here for a permit: **https://canypermits.nps.gov/**

Remaining permits are given at Visitor Centers the day of the trip, up to one hour before the close of business each day.

Backcountry Hiking At-Large Sites

This area allows camping anywhere. Camping sites must be 300 feet (92 m) from any archeological, water or historic site (Indian ruins, etc.). It must be one mile (1.6 km) from any road.

From the north entry of Salt Creek to the junction of Angel Arch, four "at large" permits are available for each site. Each is valid for seven days (subject to change).

Salt Creek Area Bear Country

Black bears returned to Salt Creek when the jeep road in the canyon was closed. Fortunately, they generally avoid disgusting humans. They arrive here from the Abajo Mountains as early as mid-June, harvesting local food, especially during early fall, when berries are ripe.

Females breed every other year with cubs being born from early January to mid-February at a weight of 1/2 to 3/4 pounds (226 – 340 grams). IF you see a bear with cubs, **quickly leave** as they will kill you to protect their cubs. At 200 pounds (91 kg), you could become a source of food for her cubs.

Bear Rules

There are two major predicators in Needles; Mountain Lions and Bears. A lion track has four 'toes'; a bear has 5 'toes. As of writing, here have been no bear attacks in Needles. Canyonland's bear Internet site is: **https://www.nps.gov/cany/planyourvisit/bears.htm.** Their recommendation on a bear attack differs from that below. They use the defense posture of a grizzly bear attack. Take your choice.

1) Be vigilant and **do not**:
a) Surprise a bear by your presence. Make sounds as you travel. When approaching dense brush, stop and listen. Can you smell a dead animal that a bear may be eating?
b) If you see a bear, slowly walk in the opposite direction. IF the bear is close to you, remain still and do not stare at the bear. Calmly talk to the bear. Do not run as this will encourage an attack.
b) Threaten her cubs in any way. Slowly walk away.
c) Approach their food (carcass).

2) IF the bear <u>runs toward you</u> as if attacking:
a) Stand still – do NOT run away. They are faster.
b) Traditionally, a bear is bluffing and will stop close to you. If you run, it almost ensures a fatal attack.
c) Back away slowly, and keep watching the bear. Do not turn and run.
d) If a bear follows you, act boldly: yell, raise your arms and throw things directly at it.
3) IF actually attacked, do <u>not</u> pretend to be dead as is the case for grizzly bears. Instead, consider this the absolute fight of your life as your life depends on it. Do everything possible to defend yourself. Attack the nose and eyes with a branch, etc. How to fight a bear? A Russian victim bit the bear's tounge off causing the bear to leave.
4) Wear a bear suit from the 1800s in Siberia

25

5) Pepper Spray may be very effective (or not), but the bear must be close enough for it to be effective. Bear spray is not allowed on air planes. Spray content should be more than 225 grams. Spray distance and time of spray varies with manufacturer. Consider having two cans: one for entering and another for exiting. Watch this very important video. What if you see a bear? See 4:20 of this video to learn how to act and talk to the bear. Note: 16 feet = 2.75 seconds at 30 mph.
https://www.youtube.com/watch?v=hBjbeQSF-l0
5) Guns – By a Supreme Court Ruling you are allowed to carry guns. By Canyonland rules, you are not allowed to fire (press the trigger). If you shoot a bear, a court must decide the final decision. Best is S&W 500.

Campers at Salt Creek including Salt Horse Zone in the Needles **must store all** food, beverages, and associated containers, garbage, and all scented items in a **hard-sided and IGBC-approved bear-resistant container** at least 100-feet from camp. Depending on bear migration, Lost Canyon may also have that restriction due to water availability to the bears.

The Visitor Center has some containers to loan. These cylinder-shaped containers are about 12 inches in diameter and 12 inches high (30 by 30 cm). They can be purchased on the Internet. Search: *camping bear proof containers*.

Mountain Lion

The mountain lion is dangerous to humans; however, it is rarely seen due the animal's natural avoidance of stinking and disgusting humans. Keep small children near you.

When I see mountain lion tracks while walking in a canyon, I stay away from ledges or trees as this is the favored mode of attack to drop down on you.

If one approaches you do NOT run or "play dead" as their native instinct is to chase and capture docile prey. Stay in position and make yourself aggressive by direct eye contact, loud-calm shouting and physical actions to enhance your aggressive size and posture. Do not approach the animal as that may put the animal in a defensive posture---not recommended, as they always win.

Backcountry Improved Camping Sites

Driving times to each campground are from the Visitor Center.

> A - Horsehoof – Plan a 3-hour drive. One site for several tents, chemical toilet, picnic table and a superb panoramic view. The arch collapsed in 1999, but we have a picture of that arch. The hoof is at the bottom left end of the arch.

> B - <u>Bobby Joe</u> - Plan a 2.5-hour drive. Two sites for several tents, existing chemical toilet is schedule to be removed, good view.

> C - <u>Devils Kitchen</u> - Plan a 2-hour drive. Four sites, each with several tent sites, two chemical toilets. These are bordered by huge boulders with an excellent sunrise view of spires.

> D - <u>New Bates</u> Plan a 2.5-hour drive. (named after Needles founder) – One site.

> E - <u>Peekaboo</u> - Plan for a 45-minute drive. Two sites.

Backcountry Designated <u>Unimproved</u> Sites

> **<u>Big Springs Trail</u>** (not the overlook parking lot).

BS 1 Along trail, partial shade, hosting 2 tents;

BS 2 Along trail, partial shade, water available, hosting 2 to 3 tents.

> **<u>Chesler Park</u>** (CP) No water.

CP 1 Off trail affording no shade. Most popular.

CP 2 Along trail with some shade. Hosts two or three tents.

CP 3 Along trail with some shade. Hosts three tents.

CP 4 Along trail with no shade. Hosts four tents.

………..Between campsites 4 and 5 is Cowboy Camp.

CP 5 Along trail with some shade. Hosts four tents.

> **<u>Confluence Overlook</u>** - At large camping only.

> **<u>Devils Pocket</u>** (South of Devils Kitchen) No water.

DP-1 Along trail

> **<u>Elephant Canyon</u>**

EC-1 – Most Popular site – Reserve ASAP.

EC-2 – Prized site on flat sandstone with superb view of Chesler Park in the distance.

EC-3

> **Lost Canyon**
LC-1 Brush, some shade, no view, no water.
LC-2 Off trail with some shade from boulders, good view.
......Water should be available in the wash.
LC-3 Near trail with shade by dwarf pines. Water should be available in the main wash.

Lower Red Lake– (Map shows as Red Lake) At large camping only from junction. See hiking trail map further down in text.

Salt Creek Canyon – The south entry is preferred to avoid a steep climb up to the Trailhead if you entered from the north. The southern Trailhead entry is on BLM land where you can camp anywhere.

After descending a very steep, rocky, 300 yards (275 m) (estimate) on the trail, the trail turns west. After an estimated 800 yards, a sign indicates the park border.

Thereafter, camping is allowed by permit only.

SC-1 & 2 – At the far south end of the trail. Off main trail east of Kirks Cabin, brush area with shade provided by large boulders, good water source.

SC-3 - Site visible from trail in an open area with good views. Potential water source nearby.

SC- 4 It is visible from the trail with shade from large Cottonwood trees.

Water may be stagnant in the summer. There are no designated campgrounds; therefore, it is an *at large* camp area where you can camp anywhere known as Salt/Horse Zone. Suggest camping near Angel's Arch. Try to find a site that has been used. Leave that area pristine as if no one was there – not even a mouse.

Note: This area is classified as bear country, requiring bear proof food containers as explained earlier.

Squaw Canyon (SQ)
SQ-1 Some shade, no view, with water.
SQ-2 Near trail with partial shade from dwarf pine, short walk to view points with water.

- **Horse Canyon** – Not shown on trail maps. Four at-large permits, no water.
- **Davis & Lavender Canyons** - Not shown on trail maps. Two at-large sites.

6.0 Hiking

Hiking is the primary and **best** mode to enjoy the landmarks of this park. Chesler Park is the most popular area. Strenuous Lower Red Lake Trail ends at the Colorado River.

Needles Park hiking is often on shallow to deep sand; therefore, wear shoes that cover high above the ankle to mitigate sand in your shoes. From mid-June to September, these canyons are very hot.

Depending on bug concentration, wearing shorts may be prohibitive.

Suggest wearing oversized pants <u>hung loosely</u> by suspenders <u>without a belt</u> to allow free flow of air to cool your body.

Guide to USGS maps

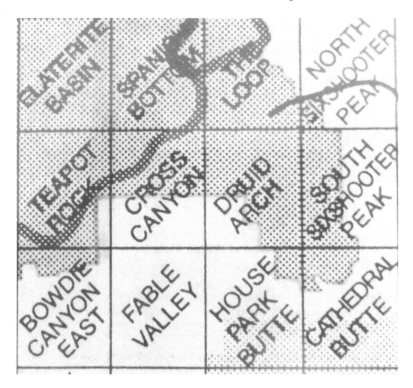

Note: These maps are available in xxx.pdf format. In your search bar, type in: USGS Map – *then the name* – pdf.

Maps for Needles hiking:
USGS: 7.5 min: The Loop Utah and Druid Arch.

Hiking and Driving Map

The map below shows the maze of trails in this park. Obviously, there is no best route; however, most hikers start from Elephant Hill Parking lot.

Note: While large, Elephant Hill parking lot fills very early in the morning. Suggest hiking up the trail about 100 yards to a narrow slot with stair steps – excellent tourist photograph.

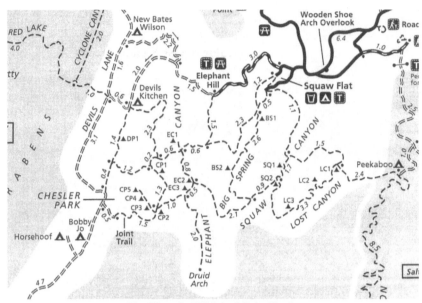

Trailheads Within Main Park

There are five Trailheads in Needles:

1. Elephant Hill
2. Squaw Flat (Campgrounds A and B)
3. Joint Trail (Off Elephant Hill Road)
4. Peekaboo
5. Big Springs parking lot for Confluence Trail and Slickrock Loop.

Trail	Miles	Km	HRs	T	W
Chesler Park Viewpoint	6	10	3-4	X	
Big Spring to Squaw Canyon	7.5	12	3-4	X	X
Squaw Canyon to Lost Canyon	8.7	14	4-6	X	X
Confluence Overlook	10	16.5	5-6		
Peekaboo	10	16.5	5-6	X	X
Big Spring Cny to Elephant Canyon	10.8	17	4-6	X	X
Druid Arch	11	18	5-7	X	
Chesler Park Loop with Joint Trail	11	18	5-7	X	

* All distance is round trip.

Cyn – Canyon; T – Toilet at Trailhead; W – Water at Trailhead

Lower Red Lake to Colorado River

From	Miles	Km	Time	Elev
Elephant Hill Parking	19	31	Overnight	1900/488
Devils Lane Road	10	15	6-8 Hours	

Salt Creek (one way) – Read Bear Rules

From	Miles	Km	Time
Peekaboo Entry	22	35	2-4 nights
Cathedral Butte	22	35	Same
Angel Arch Trailhead From Peekaboo	11.3	18	Overnight

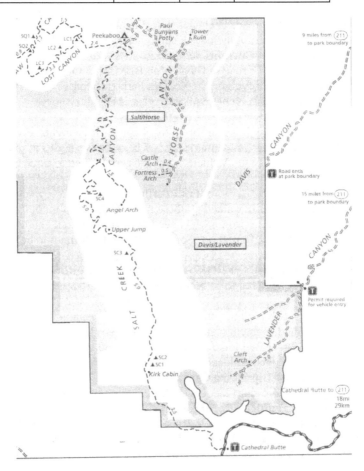

Permits Required

Day-use permits are required for Elephant Hill, Peekaboo/Horse Canyon and Lavender Canyon when IN the park boundary. Overnight camping permits are required everywhere in Needles Park. Suggest applying for a campsite at least four months in advance for spring and fall seasons; especially in Chesler Park.

Depending on time availability by the staff, the Visitor Center may be open until 4:00 PM. High demand periods are during cool spring and fall months. Day permits are available 24 hours before entry and up to one hour before closing time.

As of this writing, there is no fee for a permit.

Fortunately, a backcountry permit does not reduce quantity of day-use permits. For overnight permits, see camping section.

Quantity of Permits per Day

Needles Park restricts access via a permit system. Day pass permit quantity is shown below (subject to change). **Note:** The definition of a vehicle includes off-road licensed motorcycles.

1) Elephant Hill: Vehicles = 24. Bicycles = 12.

2) Salt Creek (Peekaboo)/Horse Canyon. Vehicles = 10. Bicycles = 7. Road into Horse Canyon is gated. Your entry permit includes a combination to that lock.

3) Lavender Canyon roads. Vehicles = 8. Bicycles = 7. Road into Lavender Canyon is gated. Your permit includes a combination to that lock.

4) Lower Red Lake – 5 permits per day.

5) Davis Canyon - The road to Davis is on BLM land. Once at the park border, entering the canyon requires a normal Needles Park entry pass.

6) Beef Basin permit is **NOT** required as that is BLM territory.

Length of Stay

Overnight permits may be valid for up to 14 consecutive nights. For backpacking at-large zones, maximum stay is 7 consecutive nights at one site, then you must move to another site. Vehicle camp sites are limited to three consecutive nights.

Trail Difficulty

Note: We have **not** fully walked all these trails. Data for those other trails has been obtained by talking to people who have journeyed that trail and/or coupled with park and tour book information. Consequently, all information below serves as **a guide, not fact**.

The numbers represent **ROUND TRIP** (unless noted).

Most trails are considered to be moderately difficult. Four are strenuous. These are:

-From Elephant Hill parking lot to the top;

-A sand/deep sand segment in a canyon to Druid Arch;

-From end of Lower Red Lake Trail to the Colorado River and back; 4) Steep climb while exiting at the south end of Salt Creek Trail.

-Slickrock Trail by Big Spring Canyon is the easiest.

Many trails have short ladders to climb/descend from one level to the other.

Salt Creek may **require several wet creek crossings,** especially after a snow melt. The trail to the Colorado/Green River confluence is mostly over flat ground.

The most scenic area is Chesler Park; therefore, those campsites are very difficult to reserve. Only major trails are described, not the endless branches of trails.

Arches

There are many arches in the park. **Druid Arch** is the most scenic and popular followed by Angel. Druid was first discovered by Bates and Alan Wilson while flying over the area in a airplane. For several summers, people failed to find it on the ground leading to its name as the Lost Arch. In 1959 Alan Wilson, his father and others were exploring the area when Alan found it.

The Druid Arch name was given by Alan's cousin, Robert Dechert, who saw its photograph and thought of Stonehenge, England builders.

Angels Arch off Salt Creek Hike. **Castle** and **Fortress Arches** are located at the end of Horse Canyon. **Cleft Arch** is located at the end of Lavender Canyon. There is a secluded Indian ruin near that arch.

YouTube: Select a trail and search the Internet for a video of that trail.

Landmark Map: This is a remarkable trail design of all Needles Park's landmark. Zoom in/out using your mouse. To the right is a list of the landmarks that correlate with those labels shown on the map.

https://caltopo.com/m/0QJ0

Trail Descriptions

Caution: There are rattlesnakes in this area, including the faded Midge Rattlesnake that is very poisonous. Fortunately, it has a small mouth and is very timid. Always be alert for a rattle noise warning. Remember: snakes cannot back up.

Basic rule: Do NOT put a hand or foot where you can't see its placement. People with walking sticks should 'tap' the ground to alert a snake of your presence – don't surprise them.

Angel Arch – This is a 1.5-mile (2.4 km) trail off Salt Creek Trail on a former road. The base of the arch is 45-feet and the height is 105+ feet (14m x 32m). The hike from the canyon bottom to the base of the arch is tedious, but not strenuous.

Big Spring to Squaw Canyon - Trailhead is at Squaw Flat 'A' Campground. This very scenic trail meanders over large sandstone slickrock and drops down/up connecting two steep canyons that offers an attractive view of Needles landscapes.

The trail is a challenge to those who are timid of narrow trails and steep cliffs.

Avoid the trail if wet, because it becomes very slippery.

Big Spring to Elephant Canyon – This very scenic trail meanders across vast slickrock to the top of mesas looking down into canyons coupled with panoramic views. Sheer cliff walls are the prize. Two ladders must be climbed.

Cave Spring Loop – Trailhead is at the end of the road. The loop is only 900 yards long. The cowboy camps are hidden under rock overhangs with replicated cowboy camping fixtures. A typical wooden grain storage box is shown along the trail.

Notice the tin can nailed between boards to prevent rodents from eating through the wood joints. Next is a large alcove with a weeping water spring. Near the trail is a metate rock with three oval shaped depressions used by Indians to grind corn. Presumably across this rock is a pictograph that we could not find.

Chesler Park – Also known as *The Needles*. This is the premier scenic walking tour of the park. It is about 1,500 yards in diameter. It was an excellent cattle grazing area.

EC 1 is the absolute most popular camp site. Thus, early camping reservations are mandatory. Chesler Park is a large meadow bordered by geologically colorful, dominant, red/white/pink Cedar Mesa Sandstone monoliths, providing panoramic colorful scenes, especially at sunrise. The picture below was taken in the proximity of EC2 on the park trail map.

Chesler Park Trail - from Elephant Hill parking lot. Initial hike is up a strenuous trail to the top. Along the trail there are narrow channels with small irritating boulders that must be crossed.

4-WD Driving - From Elephant Hill parking lot drive approximately 8 miles (13 km) to Joint Trail parking lot. From this parking lot, it is a 1.5-mile (2.4 km) hike one-way trail to an overlook of Chesler Valley.

The hike passes through Joint Trail, which is a mystically narrow (about 300yards long) slot canyon. See Joint Trail description below.

Chesler Wash Pictograph Panel – *Marching Men*. The author discovered this panel by pure random luck while resting under a pine shade tree.

From the Chesler (Joint Trail) parking lot, go up the hill on the Joint Trail.

Then, after about 30 yards, there is a 5-foot (1.5 m) high pine tree at N38 06.212 W109 51.957. Look right for a very faint road as shown in the map further below under *Virgina Park* hiking. Depending on the route chosen, after about 1.3 miles, you will see this rock formation from the wash to the left.

Video: https://youtu.be/Mf54sMU0sxc

Walk to the tall pine in the center (center bottom above), then left of the tree to the pictograph panel. N 38 05.716 W 109 51.133.

This alcove is about 10 feet wide (3 m). DO NOT enter, touch, add, modify or breathe on this ancient art panel. Please preserve it.

The multitude of hands is overwhelming. However, it is the marching men that are fascinating.

Just like the Procession Panel (Book 4, Tour 2-04-01), these men appear to have a purpose. There is the upper and lower panel. Both have a 'U' shaped object that is the focus of their attention. That is, they appear to pause at the image, contemplate and continue on their procession.

The men appear to be marching right to left until they reach that object.

When finished, walk to the back of the canyon for this pictograph. The Shaman (priest) figure is obvious as is the bird image. The image to the left could be the image of a woman, ? and then a man.

Confluence of Colorado & Green River

The Green River originates in western Wyoming. The Colorado was originally named Grand River that flows 750 miles (1,170 km) to meet the Green River at this location. The name was formally changed to Colorado by an act of Congress on 25 July 1921, and confirmed by a name change by the State of Colorado.

Other than trapper D. Julien, John Powell was the first white man to camp there from 16 to 20 July in 1869, during his historic river exploration. There they rested, repaired their boats and reorganized their supplies.

He wrote:
We row around into the Grand and camp on its northwest bank; and here we propose to stay several days, for the purpose of determining the latitude and longitude and altitude of the walls.

They also camped there during their second voyage from September 16-20, 1871. In 1914, the area was surveyed as a potential site for a river dam. Many people tried to establish a tourist facility there, but none were successful due to limited tourist traffic.

River map courtesy of Wikipedia.

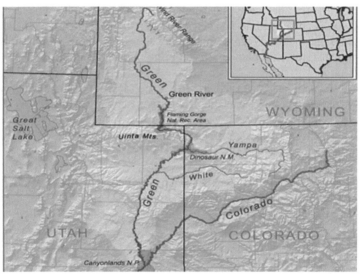

The Green River enters from the left and Colorado from the right. Notice the two shades of the water color. Colorado, in Spanish, translates to the color red.

Hiking - The trail originates at Big Spring Canyon, and crosses open country to the confluence, 1,000 feet (305 m) below.

Driving from Visitor Center - See Tour 1-03-01.

Driving from Elephant Hill – From Devil's Garden junction, it is a 6-mile (10 km) drive to the trailhead. The hike is about 800 yards.

Druid Arch – The trail passes by spectacular views of the Needles. The last 500 yards in the canyon is on deep sand. The last 400-yards to the arch base is a steep climb that includes one ladder. Wear good gripping shoes. This bold arch is shown in many tourist magazines. Best photographed during mid-morning.

Note: From Joint Trailhead, off Elephant Hill Road to Druid Arch, it is a 5-mile (8 km) one-way hike. Water may be available during the cooler seasons.

Joint Trail – This is not really a trail, but a narrow slot on the trail to Chesler or Druid Arch Trails.

No trip photograph album is complete without passing through this slot. Backpack is shown on the canyon floor. At the end there are about 25 steps that exit the slot onto a view of Chesler Park.

Lost Canyon Loop Trail – This is a popular trail due to contrasting scenery from low water pools to steep cliffs. Short sections may be considered relatively strenuous. There are multiple entries into the Loop Trail as shown on the map.

Ladders must be climbed from one level to another.

Water is normally present in pools or a flowing creek that should be filtered. Consequently, it was a favored grazing area for cattle. Confirm water availability at the Visitor Center. This water creates pleasant riparian areas, that hosts wildlife. In these areas, colorful walls and tall Cottonwood trees and/or a Willow canopy offers shade and a nice photographic contrast.

The trail varies from sandy to slickrock. When on slickrock, there should be rock cairns. Always look ahead for the next cairn before leaving the present cairn.

Lower Red Lake – Strenuous 4-mile (6.4 km) one-way hike with a 1,600+foot (488 m) elevation change. Maximum slope reaches 19 degrees. Allow at least 5 hours. Trail was rehabilitated in the mid1960s.

Legend relates this was a route used by Butch Cassidy's gang after a bank or train robbery. His crime career started in 1894 and continued to 1908 where, presumably, he was shot dead in Bolivia, South America.

From Monticello, they passed through Needles and down this canyon to the river. At the river, they turned upstream to Spanish Bottom and then up to the mesa (currently a hiking trail to Doll House). Then westward via Standing Rocks to the Dirty Devil River (now a 4-wheel drive road) then to their various hideouts that are identified in Book 2, *Escalante to Moab, Utah*. Book 1 visits his cabin where he was raised.

Hiking: A 15-foot (4.6 m) rope is beneficial to lower your backpack at various dry-falls. It is very hot during summer. There is no lake unless it has rained; otherwise, it is a large dry sand area. Trailhead is located on Devils Lane where Elephant Hill Road from Devils Kitchen merge. The 4.8-mile (7.7 km) trail ends at the river at about 3.5+ miles (5.6 km) south of the confluence of Green and Colorado Rivers onto a sandy beach. Invasive non-native Tamarisk brush must be combated to reach the river. Downstream about 0.7 miles (1.1 km) is the beginning of Cataract Canyon, (canyon is 46 miles (74 km) long), famous for its wild rapids

The view across the river is the Canyonlands-Maze District.

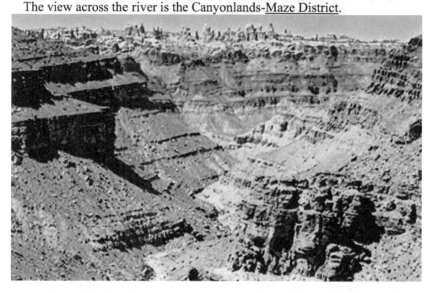

The trail begins at Devils Lane, as shown in the map below. It is the only reasonable route to the Colorado River from Needles.

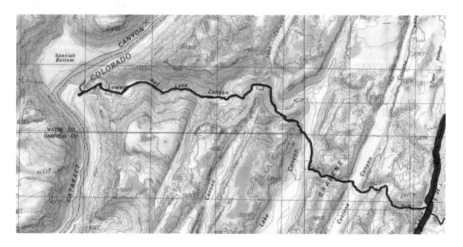

There is no water along this trail. Therefore, it should be an overnight trip. Expect Colorado river water to be muddy/silt making it difficult to filter. This is a classic deep narrow canyon strenuous trail that follows an old obstructed road down a steep canyon. At the river, a crude 3.5-mile (5.6 km) trail north goes to the river confluence. Across the river is Spanish Bottom, located in the Maze District (Book 2). Spanish Bottom is an amazing aberration, dropping from a steep canyon where it becomes a flat 120-acre (49 ha.) area on the west side of the river. Main Cataract Canyon rapids are about 4 miles (6 km) downstream.

Peekaboo Springs from Squaw Campground

Along the route, crossing both Squaw and Lost Canyons, there are several ancient granary ruins tucked into a cliff. This trail starts across a sand mesa and then climbs steeply up slickrock ending at Salt Creek Canyon Trailhead. The trail is on high slickrock rims providing scenic panoramic views. Two ladders must be climbed.

Lost Canyon Cowboy Camp - It was owned by Scorup-Sommerville Cattle Company from 1919 to the late 1960s, when it was transferred to Needles Park.

Of historical interest is that cowboys used to bury food along their intended trail. They would first dig a hole in soft sand and put their food in the hole. Then they would cover it with a tarpaulin that would protect the food for at least three years. When mice or rats tried to dig down to the food, the sand would flow back down faster than they could dig it out, thereby protecting their food supply. That food had to be kept away from any alcove as that would attract moisture.

Water was precious and often found in rock depressions. Here, a creek affords a water source. The typical diet of a cowboy was pinto beans, flour and salt pork without dessert.

Drive on Salt Creek Road to a metal gate that restricts entry into the 4-Wheel drive Horse Canyon road and park there. Walk to the immediate west into the wide sandy wash as shown in the map below. The camp can be identified when the canyon narrows to about 150-yards. One-way distance is 2.4 miles (3.9 km)

On the east side of the wash, there are cedar fence posts with rusting old barb wire. The campground is located west of the creek from GPS N38 07.692 W109 46.325 (ledge west of the alcove). The map below shows the approximate location of the camp at the bottom left. Trail starts at the Horse Canyon parking lot.

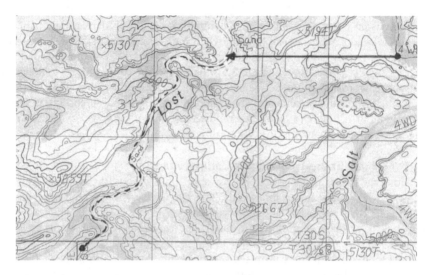

This is the landmark for Cowboy camp located at the bottom alcove behind the trees.

There are two parts in this alcove: the kitchen and, to the right, a panel with many cowboy writings. Imagine living here for months tending to cattle including hot summers

Inside this alcove is a small kitchen and two 55-gallon (208 l) drums of oats for horses. One had its cover eaten by a rat. Unfortunately, the rat could not escape and his skeletal remains are still there. The other drum is about ¾ full, having some rodent droppings. See Medical Appendix for Hantavirus carried by rodents.

Some of the cans still have food in them. Empty glass quart jars are piled in a corner as are many empty cans, especially MJB brand coffee cans, baking powder and a Skoal chewing tobacco can.

On our first visit, a pair of worn pants were hung over a pole as if it was left to dry. Also, of unique historical interest, written in capital letters, was this paper wanted poster:

Wanted for ??blurred??
Weight 180
Complexion Black
Approach with caution
   Negro Bill (replaced the offensive term used in that era)
Alias W. G. Jaupe
$5000 Reward for information leading to the arrest of this man
   Signed - J. Edgar Hoover. (Note: He was in office March 1935 to May 1972)

To the right of the kitchen is another joining alcove. Inside, graffiti dates from 1917 to 1943. Spanish language also appears to be written by J. E Trujillo: *Este dia de hoy tengo* (*This day I have*) and *El mal parada* (*the bad stop or bad job*). Another writes: *This is hell of a job working among the ---old ---* There are profiles of Negro Bill drawing with dark axel grease recommending that he should be hanged.

Book 2, *Escalante, Utah to Moab Utah,* has a lengthy background of this wanted poster in Moab section – Negro Bill Canyon.

Another section has a sketch of an Indian woman and man with two 6-shooter pistols and a rifle pointing at them.

Salt Creek - Upper and Lower– In our opinion, this is a mandatory hike to appreciate the ancient Anasazi culture that lived in this canyon. It is not as scenic as Chesler Park, but that is not the purpose of this hike. A minimum of two camping nights is recommended.

Maps: Cathedral Butte (South trailhead to Wedding Ring Arch) **Druid Arch** (Remainder of trail)

Preserve all ruins and ancient rock art (pictographs and petroglyphs) by **not touching** or walking in or on them, etc. Your finger's salt and oils accelerate their destruction. The premier and historically precious pictograph is named the *All American Man* found in Salt Creek.

Total one-way distance is 22-miles (35 km). USGS maps are: Cathedral Butte, South Six-shooter Peak and Druid Arch. Obviously, if one -were to walk the entire canyon, a vehicle at either end would be most appropriate. There are four authorized campsites as shown on the map.

This area was placed on the National Register of Historic Places in 1975. The approved 6 January 1995 Canyonlands Background Management Plan allowed the existing road to remain open to Angel Arch junction that is about 10-miles (16 km) from the current northern trailhead. The road then continued to Angel Arch. A Salt Lake City environmental group sued the park to the effect it was negligent in preserving that area for future generations. On 23 September, Judge Dale Kimball of the Federal 10th District Court ruled the canyon be closed to vehicles under case 2:95:CU 5599. It was upheld on appeal in 2000.

An ample supply of water, coupled with flat land for farming lured many ancient Anasazi Indians into this area. They left behind splendid ruins and rock art. After the Indians abandoned this area, cattle ranchers invaded – alas. When this area became a park, those cattle were removed.

Northern entry has some fascinating pictographs as shown below. This bold panel was painted at the trailhead by the Fremont Indians between 1000 and 1300 A.D. These images were painted over much older art painted by the Archaic People who lived in Canyonlands at least 1,000 to 3,000 years earlier. This older artwork is very faint, but it is still distinguishable from the newer Fremont art.

Water is normally flowing in the creek but confirm at the Visitor Center. There are no cattle in this area; therefore, water is relatively safe, but filtering is always safer. Be prepared for many creek crossings.

An ideal *at large* camp site is about 100 yards north of Angel Arch junction.

Unique to Needles are 'faces' pictographs. The 4-faces pictograph is next to the trail. Others are scattered within Needles. The other charismatic pictograph is the *All American Man*. **Note:** The only other park that has *faces* is at Pink Sand Dunes near Kanab, Utah, described in Book 3, *Vermilion Cliffs National Monument*. Most of the Anasazi Indian ruins are located south of the junction to Angel Arch, thereby favoring entry from Cathedral Butte. A set of 10 to 20 power binoculars is highly recommended because current rules do not allow anyone to be closer to an archeological (ruin) site than 300-feet (91m) (it keeps expanding).

These are details of the Salt Creek hike from south to north using the trailhead at Cathedral Butte, Tour 1-03-05 at mile 17.7.

Videos:
Day 1 **https://www.youtube.com/watch?v=X1TvM5qiJnk**
Day 2 **https://www.youtube.com/watch?v=yiX6brLl5Ww**
Day 3 **https://www.youtube.com/watch?v=QDiQtivGsYw**
Day 4 **https://www.youtube.com/watch?v=8BijWIeCTXc**
Day 5 **https://www.youtube.com/watch?v=I_v6cVz969k**

This is a **virtual 360 degree** of the hiking trail through Salt Creek
https://www.hikingproject.com/trail/7014712/salt-creek-canyon-trail

Landmark Map: This is a remarkable trail design of all Needles Park's landmark. Zoom in/out using your mouse. To the right is a list of the landmarks that correlate with those labels shown on the map.

https://caltopo.com/m/0QJ0

Entry from the South off Beef Basin Road

NOTE:
> All mileage listed below is an estimate – **not fact**.
> GPS data below is at the site, unless it is noted as *at the trail*.
> GPS readings are ours unless stated as *estimated*.

> We have listed ruins and rock art that we located.
There are substantially more ruins – be alert.

M 0.0 Starting from Cathedral Butte Trailhead at N37 57.012 W109 42.368. See Tour 1-03-05, mile 17.7. Elevation at top is about 7,075-feet (2,156 m) and at the canyon bottom it is about 6,000-feet (1,828 m). The first 200+ yards is a controlled fall.

M2.5 Ruin 1 N37 58.514 W109 44.522 (trail about 500-yards east). This is a marsh with tall reeds. It was once a major grass growing area harvested by Lee Kirk for cattle hay. Somewhere here is a horse drawn hay rake. M 3.4 Next to the trail is a tiny picturesque waterfall.

M 3.5 **Lee Kirk Cabin**, wagon and corral. Lee was born in Michigan in 1859 and later worked in Colorado where he learned cattle ranching. Sometime around 1886, he purchased some cattle and grazed them at Indian Creek (Dugout Ranch area) as did many other small ranchers. In the early 1890s, he moved his herd here and "Desert squatted" (informal homesteading without legal standing) on 80-acres (32 ha.) of land.

During winter, his family lived in Moab so his children could attend school while he tended his cattle. In the summer they lived in this cabin. Lee transitioned from cattle to sheep herding by moving his sheep to east of Moab. By 1918, this vacated land became the property of Al Scorup's Ranch.

Some of the cabin's hand axe hewn logs are almost 20-inches (51 cm) thick and four inches (10 cm) wide, all on a rugged stone foundation. Notice the many deer antlers indicating a vital food source.

The 100+ year old wagon was pulled by horses hauling supplies from Moab at least twice each year. Lee died in 1945, but his durable cabin stands as testimony to those rugged small ranchers of this area. Do NOT enter as there may be deadly Hanta Virus in the cabin.

If not rotted, you may see a sample of his wooden fence. Rather than use crossed poles to hold a horizontal pole, he elected to drive two poles in the ground. Then inserted a wood peg through both posts upon on which a horizontal pole was secured. Exceptionally labor intensive.

When this area became part of the park in 1964, an agreement was made allowing for ten-years of grazing rights (common process) to its former owners. After those ten years, the Park offered to purchase the land at $132 per acre and if not accepted, they would threaten the owner with condemnation of the land—zero dollars.

A December 1976 court challenge brought a reasonable solution: $1,400 an acre.

M 3.7 **Campgrounds SC1 and SC2.**

M ?? Kirk's Arch has a span of 165-feet (50 m). It is located about one-mile (1.6 km) west on top of the mesa. It can only be seen intermittently in the distant horizon. It is almost impossible to climb to it. Estimated location: N37 59.487 W109 45.600.

M 4.1 Ruin 2- east side about 75-yards off the trail – N37 59.482 W109 44.327.

M 4.8 **Big Pocket** Canyon to the southeast. There are several ruins, two of which require ladders to enter. The first ruin is 300 yards from the trail on the south side. The best ruin is slightly over one mile east from the trail also on the south side facing east. The third is almost one mile further to the northeast. We don't have GPS data for those ruins.

M 5.0 Ruin 3 **Big House Ruin** - N38 00.103 W109 44.465 (at trail). About 700 yards west of the trail is the largest ruin in the entire Canyonlands Park system, including the Maze and Island in the Sky.

This village has about 20 rooms in a 100yard long cliff alcove. Black soot remains on the ceiling. This is a typical defensive village next to sheer 30-foot (9 m) walls, requiring long ladders for access.

The trailhead marker to these is a large diamond-shaped boulder about 15-feet (4 m) high located north of Big Pocket Canyon. Continue north about 60 yards past this rock to the actual trail.

M ?? Wedding Ring Arch is 200-feet high and 150-feet wide (61 by 45 m) located to the right of the trail. It is almost a perfect circle; hence, the name.

Depending on where you are, it may not be visible from the trail, requiring you to 'hunt' for it. Estimated at N37 58.665 W109 43.958.

M ? Ruin foundation N38 00.451 W109 44.440 (trail – 200-yards east of trail).
M ? Ruin 4 N38 00.706 W109 44.560 (trail – about 200-yards west in a cove).
M ? Ruin 5 – east side N38 00.883 W109 44.473.
M ? Ruin 6 N38 00.907 W109 44.674 (trail) – Located about 500 yards east 1/2 way up canyon wall. Small village.

M 5.3? **Fisheye Arch** to the distant east, located about one mile north of Wedding Ring Arch. Estimated at N38 00.442 W109 43.590.
M ? Ruin 7 N38 01.171 W109 44.914 – West of trail about 30-yards. This is a very unique site as the three ruins (probably granaries) are at ground level. About 50-yards west along the same level is a large stone with five metate grooves. Each groove was used to grind grain (corn) using another rock –named mano.
M ? Ruin 8 -East side - N38 01.340 W109 44.812. Pictographs (shaman). Another ruin further north about 200-yards.
M ? Ruin 9 N38 01.487 W109 45.008 - Hand print west of trail about 15-yards.
M ? Ruin 10 N38 02.xxx W109 44.710. Granaries (Antler ruin). There is one ruin at the entrance to the canyon and two more ruins back into a small canyon about 50-yards.

M 8 ? Ruin 11 N38 02.120 W109 44.926. The **All-American Man** is located in a small narrow cave about 15-feet (4.6 m) above the ground.
It was painted by the Fremont Culture. White outline was added by an unknown photographer. Stone ruins are of Anasazi origin. There are some small granaries east of this landmark in northern canyons.

48

M ? <u>Ruin 12</u> North-northeast about 500-yards in alcove. N38 02.219 W109 45.297 (at trail).

M ? <u>Ruin 13</u> Small ruin west of trail about 100-yards under boulder alcove (across from 4 Faces). N38 02.318 W109 45.728 (west of waterfall).

M ? <u>Ruin 14</u> Large ruin at ground level east of trail about 20-yards.

Also the 700+ year old **4 Faces** pictograph next to the trail. Do not TOUCH! This ruin is near a small waterfall. N38 02.380 W109 45.596.

M 8 ? **Campground SC 3 to the west.**

M ? Ruin 15 N38 02.501 W108 45.887 – Two Faces.

M 89 **Upper Jump** N38 02.588 W 109 45.878. This is another small waterfall where a small pond creates a pleasant shaded area by Cottonwood trees. The canyon narrows and becomes very dense with vegetation for about two miles. Be very vigilant of where the main trail is located. People inadvertently walk off the trail creating false trails.

M 10+ Large ruins located about 30 yards above valley floor. There are approximately 15 ruins here composed of apartments and storage granaries. Pictographs are found at the western side of the ledge. There is a procession of about 200 human images, holding each other's hands.

M 10.8 Junction of Salt Canyon with West Fork Canyon to the west.

M 12 **SC 4 Campground.**

M 14 Junction to **Angel Arch** trail that was an old jeep road There are a couple of ruins at this junction. About 100 yards north is a select camping area under Cottonwood Trees. Most hikers camp here and hike to the arch the following morning.

To visit Angel Arch, walk on this road approximately 1.5 miles (2.4 km). Then continue on a 400-yard trail to an overlook of the arch. If you are a proficient rock scrambler, continue to the base of that arch. See Paragraph 6.0 – Hiking for a photograph and description of this arch.

M 15 Crescent Arch to the east. There is a small granary ruin within 200 yards of the trail on the way to the arch.

M 22 +/- A trail branches off the main road to Peekaboo Trailhead that will save ½ mile (800 m) of walking. The road also goes to Peekaboo. M 22.5 End of trail at **Peekaboo Trailhead**/Campground.

End of Salt Creek Hike
* *

Slickrock Loop Trail –Various views of Big Spring Canyon and, if lucky, Big Horn Sheep. Trailhead is at Big Spring Canyon Overlook, off the main road

Squaw Canyon to Lost Canyon Loop Trail - A nature hike through den vegetation which may be occasionally wet. One ladder must be climbed.

Squaw Valley Loop - Cross flat riparian area until Squaw Valley Loop junction is met.

Virginia Park – This area never experienced cattle; therefore, it remains pristine. Entry is from Joint Trail via Chesler Canyon. It is currently closed for all hikers. Each year, during the fall season, a lottery is held to select ten people for a Ranger led day hike into that area. Register at the Backcountry office. The dots show an abandoned road to that park entry. Occasionally, some road asphalt remains in the wash. USGS 7.5 map: Druid Arch.

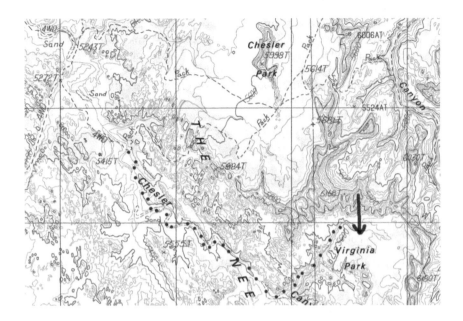

7.0 Other Tours

<u>Mountain Biking</u> - Must stay on existing roads. This is an excellent alternative to Elephant Hill backcountry. Several backcountry roads have deep sand as identified in the appropriate tour.

<u>Airplane Tour</u> – These are offered at Monticello airport.

8.0 Driving Tours

Davis, Horse and Lavender Canyons are not friendly to mountain bikes due to sand. Backcountry canyon 4-Wheel drive roads are impassable during winter. Access to Salt Creek/Horse Canyons may be flooded in the spring, making that route impassable.

Caution - Horse, Lavender and Davis Canyons. During the wet seasons, sand on these roads may convert into quicksand (water forced from the bottom) that could become dangerous depending on the size and volume of that quicksand. Always inquire at the Visitor Center for recent road conditions.

Four-Wheel Drive, High Clearance Roads

There are over 40-miles (64 km) of 4-Wheel drive trails in the park. A 4-Wheel drive vehicle can be rented in Moab, Utah. It must have a dual range speed transmission. Alternately use a mountain bike or an off-road motorcycle (street legal with license). If your vehicles breaks, towing costs can easily exceed $1,500.

    1. Elephant Hill - **DANGER** - If you are **NOT** experienced with 4-Wheel drive vehicles on very <u>steep and rough</u> roads, do **NOT** drive on Elephant Hill. Vehicles have flipped over the rim on this road. Mountain Bikes are a major challenge and should be walked up and down. Low range 4-Wheel drive is <u>mandatory</u>. Long wheel base vehicles should not attempt this drive. For example, long bed pickup trucks with extended cabs.

    2. Colorado Overlook – Moderate. After 5.5-miles (8.8 km), a rough rock stair step is encountered. Depending on vehicle clearance, it may be advisable to park here and hike the final 1.5-miles (2.4 km).

3. Horse/Peekaboo Canyons – Entry permit required. Initially expect to drive across water. Spring snow melt may close the road. Most of road from the gate is from sand to deep sand. Not suitable for Mountain Biking.

4. Davis Canyon – Entry permit required. As above, except there may be **water puddles at about 2.8-miles** (4.5 km) from gate entry where, after a rain, clay becomes impassable - exceptionally slippery.

5. Lavender Canyon – Entry permit required. Roads are similar to Horse Canyon above, plus a couple of creek crossings required.

6. Lockhart Road – BLM land - no permit required.

>>> Driving on Sand Road Instructions

Driving on sand at high engine RPM stresses the engine that may cause engine overheating. Monitor that gauge. When parking, try to have your vehicle face downhill. YouTube: *driving sand roads* has many videos.

First - Drive a high clearance 4-Wheel drive vehicle with very good tire treads. (at least a M&S rating – mud and snow). High clearance is necessary as wheels create a deep depression in the road that creates a very high center ridge. Not all 4Wheel drive vehicles have high clearance.

Option: *Fat Tire* type of bicycle with low tire pressure.
https://www.icebike.org/fat-tire-bike/

Second - Don't stop! Always maintain speed on a straight road. Go as fast as it is safe. Use sufficient speed to help you get through soft spots. If speed is being lost, try turning the steering wheel quickly back and forth about +/- 10 degrees.

If tires start spinning, stop immediately as the vehicle will sink lower until the undercarriage (body) is resting on sand. This results in a major shoveling problem or jacking the vehicle up.

Third - Avoid shifting, as that slight pause could cause you to stop. Plan on driving in 2nd gear continuously. This will significantly increase your gasoline consumption.

Fourth - Carry a shovel, high bumper jack and a tow cable or strap. If you are driving a pickup or light SUV, load some rocks (200+ pounds {91 kg}) or other weight in the back for traction. Otherwise the rear wheels will bounce and lose traction.

Fifth - Sand requires power to push the tires. Specifically, for diesel engines needing higher RPM/Power, **use low range 2nd or 3rd gear**. Same could apply to gas vehicles.

Sixth – If stuck, there are several options:

Buried in sand: Jack vehicle up and put sand under tires. A Farmers Jack is ideal. A simpler method is an air bag: Exhaust Jack up to 9,000 pounds lift.
https://www.extremeterrain.com/mean-mother-exhaust-jack-9000lb-8717-yj-tj-jk.html

Collect brush – normally not effective.

Use two 6-foot long carpets that may work. They tend to pile behind the wheels.

We use four 8-foot long 8x8 inch boards for front and back tires. Two for the front and two for the back tires.

Turning front wheels back and forth at constant rate
https://www.youtube.com/watch?v=_9mmajFmVcc

Tire Clamp-On Aid. This is a very clever invention that provide superb gripping power on the tire. **https://www.youtube.com/watch?v=E0XQhiSTkqc**

Winch - Generally in sand areas, there is nothing sturdy to hook a winch onto.

Sand Tire Pressure

----------4-Wheel Vehicle for Sand ----------

Lower tire pressure (PSI) extends the length of a tire on sand. Generally, tire pressure should be no lower than 20 psi for cars/SUV. Truck tire pressure should be about 40 psi although some lower it to 25 psi.

Excessively low pressure could cause damage to the tire sidewalls, slippage of the tire on the wheel or an air leakage, leading to a flat tire. Sand could also penetrate. Avoid sharp turns especially at higher speed as this may break the seal between a tire and rim.

Once back on the highway, your tires must be re-inflated to normal pressures. Low pressure causes a tire to deflect more as it rolls. That action creates internal heat that could result in tread separation or loss of control! Underinflated tires are very dangerous at highway speeds, so drive slower if you do not have a pump. A portable tire pump that operates off your cigarette lighter jack or clips to your battery can re-inflate your tires. Run your engine while inflating the tires to ensure your battery is not drained.

NOTE: Commercial Needles Outpost Visitor Center has air pressure to inflate your tires.

DANGER – If you use a tow strap, insure is rated for about 10,000-pound load. When pulling, **EVERYONE** must stay far away from the strap if it breaks.

Youtube has endless recommendation: Search: *vehicle stuck in sand*

----------Fat Tire Bicycles for Sand----------

These are designed for sand and snow travel. Tire size range from 3.8 to 5 inches (9.7 – 12.7 cm) – larger the better. **Careful**: Plus bike tires are smaller at about 2.5 inches (6.4 cm). Normal tire pressure for a Fat tire is 15-20 psi (103 – 138 kPa). When used for sand riding, pressure can be reduced to 4-8 psi (28 -55 kPa) creating a very large tire surface area to float over sand. Your weight is a factor when reducing tire pressure.

At time of publishing, the only potential rental store is Moab's *Bike Fiend* at 435 315 0002

Tour 1-03-01 - Colorado River Overlook

In addition to seeing the Green and Colorado Rivers merge, there are two sets of petroglyphs and a stunning view of a canyon with horizontal white strips.

The first 2.6 miles (4.2 km) are adequate for any high clearance vehicle; thereafter, it is a 4-Wheel drive road.

M 0.0 At the gate, where a gravel/dirt road begins. It is located past the Visitor Center.

M 2.6 In a wash where a sign declares the road is now 4-Wheel drive only. Park here near the bottom of the wash.

a. Walk west, down the wash about 50-yards where you will encounter a natural water spring which is Lower Jump Spring.

b. From Lower Jump Spring, continue down the wash another 200 yards where a cliff drops down a few hundred feet. Look to the left where there are two 10-foot (3 m) high bands of pure white 'rock' horizontally across the canyon. The white bands are either calcite or limestone. In any case, it is a startling contrast compared to other bland geological layers.

At the canyon rim, turn right and follow the canyon staying between the canyon and the ledge to the right observing that same white band. At about 400 yards, the arch is perched on the rim to the right at GPS N 38 11.695 W109 47.506

c. Return to the parking area. Look southwest for a jutting butte about 75 yards from the road. A very complex petroglyph is pecked into the rock are sheep, 4-headed 'god'- Shaman and a huge 'checkered' whale image. To the left are two painted snakes. N38 11.558 W109 47.220.

d. Back at the parking lot. Look east to locate a huge cylindrical column. Now, drop back into the wash and walk about 250 yards where it makes a sharp turn right. Walk a few more yards to where you see a faint path left to those columns.

About 50 yards west of that column is a small petroglyph under an overhang. It also has two snakes, a horned man and a person in a circle. A baby in a womb? N38 11.606 W109 46.903.

M 6.1 It becomes a moderately difficult 4-Wheel road. Park here and walk up the road about 50-yards to decide if you prefer walking another 1.5 miles to the overlook or driving across a rough rocky road.

M 7.1 Road ends at a parking lot where a 200-yard walk ends at the edge of the Colorado River before it merges with the Green at N38 12.947 W109 49.852. The rivers are almost 1,000-feet (309 m) below.

From here the two rivers combine as the Colorado River that flows south to the Gulf of Mexico.

Origin of both rivers: Colorado enters from the right. +

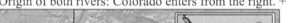

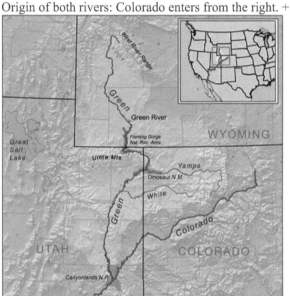

Tour 1-03-02 - Elephant Hill Road

Elephant Hill parking lot is 2.7-miles (4.3 km) from Campground "B" junction. Vehicles over 21-feet (6.4 m) long, including trailers, are prohibited on this road.

The distant southern exit is Bobby's Hole to Beef Basin (Tour 1-03-05). It may be impassable due to recent erosion. Confirm at the Visitor Center.

This is a rough 4-Wheel Drive Road with a very **nasty attitude.** It was built by cattle rancher Al Scorup in the 1940s to provide an access road to his backcountry cattle grazing lands. Wisely, he used asphalt pavement to smooth out the rough section, but most of that is now eroded.

View from top of Elephant Hill at about mile 0.5.

Unfortunately, the Park Service does not maintain this road—not even carrying a rock to fill a hole. Consequently, Elephant Hill (EH) is rated a number "7", making it one of the worst 4-Wheel drive roads in Utah. Devils Lane may have deep sand whose depth depends upon the last wind storm. Normally it is not deep.

Video from Elephant Hill to Joint Trail (Chesler Canyon Parking Lot)
Alert: Cameras are incapable of showing actual angles of decline or incline.
  https://www.youtube.com/watch?v=irT--S3QM8o
  Significant times within this video are:
  2:06 – This is a backup/turnaround area.
  8:00 - Starting down Elephant Hill. Going down is about 4X easier than up;
13:22 - Sharp turn. Turn right and back down the hill:
  16:34. At the bottom of Elephant Hill. There are many more rough areas.
  1.00:51 - This is **SOB** pass. Suggest driving down and turning right. Then back down the hill. That was not done in the video. In the video, observe their tires. It appears they have been deflated for better traction.

See *Driving on Sand Road Instruction* in Tour >>D to understand this technique.

Elephant Hill (EH) Observations.

We have been up and down three times. Twice on my motorcycle and once in our Jeep Wrangler. Our observations follow:

1. When at the Campground B Road, many Jeeps depart to Elephant Hill, but it is rare to see one return. Actually, we have never seen any vehicle return. The reason may be that they continue to Bobby's Hole to exit, avoiding the cruel backside of EH.

2. My 200 cc off road motorcycle is a delight to ride as it wound around and through the many rock obstacles of this road. The problem was returning up EH. Some sections are so steep (25 degrees +) that the center of gravity shifts to the rear wheel leaving the front tire in the air! At Bobby's Hole, a motorcycle is a challenge as that hill has very loose dirt in addition to high boulders.

Therefore, at EH, you have to ride standing up forcing YOUR weight to the front AND back wheels simultaneously. Also, a motorcycle does not favor a steep ridge (step); therefore, at times, I had to build rock piles (bridges) creating an alternate route. My suggestion is a 350 cc bike.

3. We have a Jeep Wrangler with a 2-inch lift (higher than normal) with standard tires.

  a) The 2-inch lift was adequate (with rock building). Five inches is better.

  b) Mistake with the tires. Suggest upgrading to Jeep Rubicon tires or bigger. Larger tires can ride/grip over obstacles better. This conversion requires a computer program change to odometer software. Also, off road tread like M&S (mud and snow) at a minimum.

  c) Also reduce tire pressure for greater traction by 10-15 % - your choice to give a larger 'foot' print. The lift height decreases as you expel air from your tires.

  d) Carry a large bumper jack, available from *Harbor Freight* or a 4-Wheel drive parts store. This allows you to lift the vehicle quickly and insert rocks under that tire to stop it from spinning in the air. With our Jeep, we had to build at least 15 rock ledges to raise the vehicle level to that of the obstacle, which is hard work and very time consuming.

  e) We have a 12,000-pound **winch.** The problem is that there is nothing to connect that winch to.

  f) Our round trip of driving took 11 hours due in part, to those nasty small tires!

  g) At times, our Jeep engine 'pinged' when in low engine revolution (RPM) due to hill climb problems. Suggest upgrading to the next higher octane level.

Start of Tour

M 0.0 Road starts with a steep climb from the parking lot and then crosses a flat area. At about 0.4 miles, it drops steeply to the valley bottom.

M 1.5 Junction with road from Devils Lane. Continue straight that becomes a **one-way** road.

M 3.2 Very narrow slot – Fold mirrors next to vehicle.

Devils Kitchen Junction

M 3.5 Four campgrounds to the left, with two clean chemical toilets. These secluded campgrounds do not have warm morning sunlight, but the views are memorable as the sun rises.

This is also a hiking trailhead to Chesler Park - 2.5 mi (4.0 km); Joint Trail - 4.5 mi (7.2 km); and Druid Arch - 6.8 mi (10.9 km).

Note: A **two-way** road continues to Devils Lane.
Devils Lane Junction

The wide and smooth area of Devils Lane was created by a geological phenomena, known as a Graben. It is a huge block of rock that is settling downward between two geological faults as shown below. As it flows down, it widens the surface area. This block is 900 feet (274 m) deep.

Coincidently, each side flows upwards due the pressure of the downward movement. If only one side has a fault, it is named half-Graben.

Typically, this Graben sinks about one inch (2.54 cm) each year. Devil's Lane Graben is sliding towards the Colorado River because it has the least amount of back pressure (resistance). The most popular Graben is Death Valley, California.

This Graben is estimated to be 55,000 years old. Image below compliments of NASA.

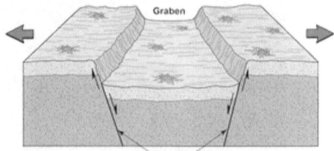

M 4.0. Devils Lane Junction - Once, this was a vast cattle grazing area where the ruins of a cowboy camp remain. One camp is located near the SOB junction.

By the quantity of ancient Indian rock art along this lane, it could have been the main route from the Colorado River (Lower Red Lake Trail) to Salt Creek or Beef Basin. Lower Red Lake Trailhead is located at Devil's Lake junction.

Touch nothing as your skin oil and salts accelerate deterioration of this delicate historic art. Do not add any graffiti.

Reset your odometer to zero and turn left.

M 0.0 Turning south towards Horsehoof Campground and Beef Basin. Depending on winds, the road can have a 6-inch (15 cm) layer of soft sand, which is brutal for Mountain Bikes and motorcycles.

M 0.1 (approximate) Lower Red Lake Trailhead to the Colorado River.

M 0.3 About 500-yards east of the road is a canyon with very well-preserved **pictographs** under an alcove. This is the most artistic and most preserved pictograph site along Elephant Hill roads. They are in the second canyon south.

The alcove is located on the left side of the canyon about 100-yards from the canyon entry at N38 08.002 W109 52.216. The images face east. It is a huge light beige colored panel. Video: https://youtu.be/t25akpckBtw

This is a very mystic site with many hands on the walls and ceilings. The ceiling panel (must lie on your back and look up) has an unusual "H" design with a large "spear" figure adjacent to it. Another section has many hand prints.

Other panels show several "shaman-priest" figures, snakes and an unusual scene where a man with a spear appears to be attacking a spirit figure. There is a very faded Kokopelli figure. The most fascinating art is its many geometric head crowns.

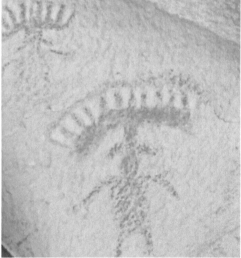

M 0.5+ There are several **pictograph** panels along the western cliffs. The first (north to south) is a very impressive shaman-anthropomorphic figure located about 35-feet (10.7 m) above the canyon floor level. This impressive panel is best viewed by binoculars. Foot access is difficult along a cliff edge.
M 38 07.943 W109 5.394.

M 1.0 About 400-yards before SOB turn, there is a short side road west that leads to a **pictograph** panel within 5-yards of the road. This 30-foot (9 m) long art panel is located at N38 07.721 W109 52.530.

It is commonly called the *Hand-Foot* panel because two-feet are painted on the panel—very unusual. These are visible to the far left. There are about 150 images on this panel dominated by hand prints. Video: https://youtu.be/4xFnXnYt9BA

Floyd Dalton decided to inscribe his own hand image and name in 1926—the first rock art destroyer. At the lower right is a pictograph severely scarred by Kent Frost. Earlier, he chiseled his name and date over an image—just for fun.

Then, Frost became one of the area's first commercial tour operators and realized that his graffiti presented a negative image to his tourists. He tried to remove his name from this art. **Sad—don't repeat his foolish mistake!**
SOB Junction

M 0.6 **SOB Pass-** While dropping only 60 feet (18.3 m), it is a short frustrating road with a very sharp turn as shown below that can be easily navigated with precautions.

From north to south, drive forward and turn right. Then back down the remainder of the slope.

From south to north, back up and drive forward up the hill. Re-arrange the hundreds of rocks as necessary. From north to south, on SOB's downhill segment, look directly left along a flat cliff wall where there are many **pictographs** of hand prints and a very faded shaman. N38 07.675 W109 52.554.

M 2.9 Junction. Turn east 0.5 miles to Joint Trail parking lot (access to Chesler Park) having a chemical toilet and a picnic bench under a shade tree. See Hiking Section for Joint Trail description. '
 That parking lot is the Trailhead for **Marching Men petroglyph**
 M 7.0 **Bobby Joe** Campground
 M 7.1 **Horsehoof** Campground 0.7 miles west.
 M 10.2 **Needles Park border**. Road continues to Bobby's Hole in Tour 103-05.

To Devil's Lane and Confluence Overlook

M 0.0 Turning north at **M 4.0 Devils Lane** junction, above. Depending on winds, the road can have a 6-inch (15 cm) layer of soft sand that is brutal for Mountain Bikes and motorcycles.
 M 0.1 To the right is an alcove where a former **cowboy camp** was located as evidenced by tin cans and a "bedroom" under a rock with a small stove. N38 08.544 W109 52.008.

Along the southwest facing wall is a faded shaman **pictograph** with two hands visible. It is located about 10-yards off the road at N38 08.572 W109 52.017.

M 1.6 **Elephant Trail junction** to the east.

This is a nasty 2.1 mile (3.4 km) one-way road to Elephant Hill road junction.

At about 1.9 miles (3 km), there is a series of rugged ledges that are known as Silver Stairs. We suggest a visual inspection of that route <u>before</u> continuing. It then continues 1.5 miles (2.4 km) up Elephant Hill and down, ending at the parking lot.

M 1.7 **Bates Wilson** Camp junction right. Bates was the original explorer of Canyonlands and its first superintendent. Thus, he is considered the Father of Canyonlands. He retired in June 1962 and became a rancher near Moab along the Colorado River.

M 5.3 **Confluence Overlook** parking lot. An easy 800-yard hike ends at a cliff.

These rivers are almost 1,000-feet (309 m) below and flow south to the Gulf of Mexico. See Tour 1-03-01, for a photograph and geological information of this confluence.

* * * * * * * * * * * * * * * * * * * ** * * ** * *

Tour 1-03-03 – To Horse Canyon via Cave Spring and Salt Creek

This tour goes to Cave Spring cowboy camp, Salt Creek Trailhead and Horse Canyon. Horse Canyon access is on the road to Cave Spring.

Cave Spring is a natural alcove was used by cowboys from the late 1890s to 1960 because it had a water seep (spring). This was the location of the original Visitor Center in August 1965. The personnel lived in the cave and trailers.

Cowboy tradition was never to empty coffee grounds from their huge coffee pot. Fresh grounds were added when fresh water was added. When coffee grounds filled the pot, it was emptied and the cycle repeated. Dutch (cast iron) pots were used to make stew where hot charcoal/wood was placed on top of the pot that radiated heat downward. Anything dead and all vegetation were added to the pot creating dinner. Notice black soot ceiling.

A precious water source is a dripping spring about 100-yards to the left of the campsite. Near the springs is an Indian *metate* and *manos* rock used for grinding corn, etc. The trail ends at a ladder, where you can climb up and continue walking across flat slickrock back to the parking lot.

To Peekaboo & Horse Canyon
M 00 At the junction before Cave Spring, turn south on Salt Creek Road

M 0.4 Large parking lot for trailhead to Lost Canyon Cowboy Cove (see hiking trails) and Horse Canyon. Vehicle entry to Horse Canyon requires a permit and a gate lock combination that is part of your permit. Write that number on a separate piece of paper as a back-up should your permit blow out the window.

After the gate, a 4-Wheel drive vehicle is required due to deep sand. Read *Driving on Sand Roads Instructions* in Tour >> D if you have not driven in sand before.

IF you get stuck in the first 2.7 miles, there is NO convenient turnaround area on this very narrow road. Towing is very expensive. Also, sections of the road squeeze through high brush that scratches the side of your vehicle.

Junction to Salt Creek and Horse Canyon
M 2.7 At this junction, turn left for 1.1-mile s(1.8 km) to a small parking lot. This is where the Salt Creek Canyon hike and Peekaboo Campground is located. See Paragraph 6.0 - Hiking in Tour >>D. Continue straight for Horse Canyon

* *

Tour 1-03-04 - Route To Horse Canyon

This is a 4-Wheel Drive Road, solely because of water in the canyon and a deep sand. If you are driving a pick-up truck, put about 200+ pounds (91 kg) of rock in the back bed for rear tire traction. **USGS Map**: South Six-Shooter Peak.

Bring binoculars to see ancient Indian ruins and arches. There may have been up to 300 people living in this canyon. If a woman survived child birth, she could have lived to fifty years; otherwise, their average age of life was in the twenties. A man survived to his thirties. The most dangerous aspect was falling off ledges, resulting in broken bones.

Miles are approximate due to tire spinning in deep sand and other factors. <u>While we believe these GPS reading are correct because of previous visits, some have not been subsequently verified due to endless access problems.</u>

<u>**These landmarks are**</u>:
M1.2 (30 Hands);
M 5.9 (13 Faces).

This canyon has a family curse on us. The first time here, it was simple. because no 4-wheel drive was required. At Bunyan Potty, there was a parking area, picnic tables and a chemical toilet. The second trip was to confirm miles and GPS. Could not enter as the road was flooded from spring snow melt. Third time the road flooded again. Fourth time, wrong type of tires for deep sand that develops at the end of summer. Fifth and final time, our GPS died at 13 faces that also affected positioning of 30 Hand Pictographs. Should you find/confirm these two sites, please confirm our GPS data and email us a photo of the Ruin and 30 Hands. We will credit you as the photographer (only the first to submit)

The map below was created from GPS tracking data; therefore, it is 100% correct. USGS 7.5-minute map is: South Six Shooter Peak Quadrangle

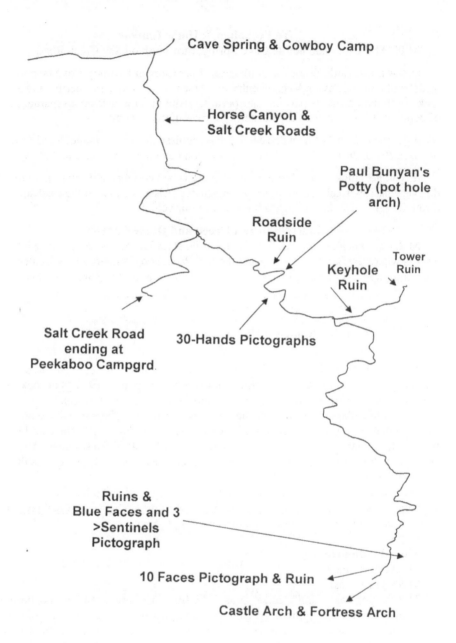

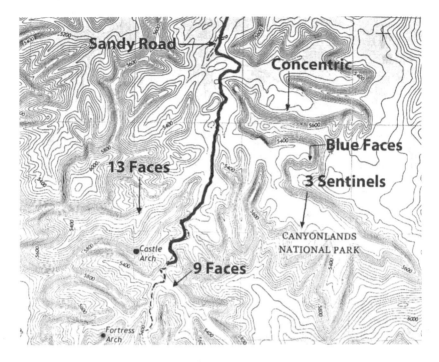

M 0.0 **From** M 2.7, Junction Salt/Horse Canyon above,
M 1.1 Behind a large bush is a well-preserved Indian ruin. N38 07.166 W109 44.341.

M 1.3 **Paul Bunyan Potty**. In the northern cliffs is a large pothole arch. A pothole arch is formed by erosion from the top, not from its side. Paul Bunyan is a huge northern Minnesota mythical lumber man and his huge ox whose massive hoof prints created Minnesota's lakes.

M 1.5 To the right is a **30-hand pictograph** about 100 yards off the road. These images are very faded. N38 07.003 W 109 44.484. Do NOT touch!

Tower Ruin Junction

M 2.2 To the left is a 0.6-mile road to Tower Ruin.

Driving to Tower Ruin: Within the first two hundred yards, Keyhole Ruin is tucked high in the cliff hole framed by a spire and the cliff. There is another ruin tucked to the left of the main ruin.

The road ends where a 300-yard walk leads to the Tower House ruins, occupied from 1120 to 1280 A.D. Tower House Ruin is spectacular because of its strategic position, ensuring its survival from erosion and any hostile attack.

Probably a single Anasazi family lived here who were seasonal farmers. Typically, these ruins were burned by those inhabitants about every 15-20 years; probably to clear it of debris, vermin and disease, since garbage was simply discarded over the cliff or on the patio. These garbage dumps are known as *middens,* a treasure for archeologists.

NOTE: The mileage below assumes you did **NOT drive** into Tower Ruin (visit after end of driving tour below)

M 3.2. Gothic Arch can be seen on top of the mesa rim.

M 5.3 **Concentric Pictograph** is located to the east in a wide canyon, identified by a large monolith butte in its center. There are 2 vertical posts blocking canyon entry at N38 04.847 W109 43.408. Back in to park. See map above for approximate location. Hike in the canyon about 125+ yards to where a dry wash merges from the right. It is a very scenic canyon with black varnish-stained beige colored walls. Follow this wash for about 600 yards to a knoll to the south. It may not be visible from the wash depending where you are located. The photograph below was taken from that knoll at N38 04.664 W109 43.163. The Circle, facing north is located at N38 04.579 W109 43.221.

It has absolutely no obvious purpose. However, about **50-yards** west of that pictograph is a small alcove with four water seeps, providing precious water to travelers. Could this image signal a water source?

It is foolish to climb there, as we did, because of a very narrow ledge that has loose rubble below it where you can easily fall to your death!

69

M 5.65 **Hand Cove pictograph, is located a**bout 15 feet (6 m) west of the road as the road takes a sharp turn. The beige-colored cove is hidden behind brush and one 20-foot-high tree. There are about 25 hands images, some very faded. N 38 04.622 W109 43.524. Do **NOT** touch these ancient fragile images!

M 5.7 **Cliff Sentinel and Blue Face Canyon.** The canyon road junction is at N38 04.580 W 109 43.526 at a shade tree where there is large parking space (in soft sand). As you walk into the canyon about 200 yards, it splits at N38 04.405 W109 43.200. Blue Faces are to the left while the Sentinels are to the right. Distance to each from the parking area is about 1,000+ yards.

Turn right and continue hiking. There is a large arch to the left at N38 04.206 W109 43.165. Look to the distant right, to the rear and, high on a cliff, where these faint Sentinels are located. They are almost inaccessible, requiring 20x powered binoculars for a detailed view. Any decent photograph requires a 300+ mm (35 mm) lens on a tripod. Three of the five Sentinel faces retain their bold colors and designs; the others are very faded. Observe the 'canes' and the lack of them in the third image which appears to be a female.

Blue Faces Pictograph Panel - Return to where the canyons split and hike to the left. As you enter this canyon, high and to the left is a huge alcove. Inside are **three cliff ruins**, visible from the canyon floor. One is very well-preserved at N38 04.434 W109 43.133. Continue to the end of the canyon and turn right (see map).

These Blue Faces are remarkable because they are blue in color, typically derived from copper not found in this area. While very highly faded, a close inspection reveals a unique hair style that is bundled on top of their heads.

At a point, about 70-yards from the pictographs, there is a faint petroglyph at N38 04.345 W109 42.998.

Blue faces are located about 100 feet (30.5 m) above the canyon floor, under an alcove overhang, near a spring. Ruins are to the right of the panel.

M 5.9 **13 Faces Pictograph Panel** This is an area of large Cottonwood trees. About 30 yards into this area, there is a parking area to the right. Park here. The topographic map above shows the location of the Faces. As shown, there are three side canyons (tiny, small and the larger) into this canyon. The Faces are in the third which is hidden behind a maze of small trees and bushes.

Following GPS has not been confirmed, but we believe it to be accurate. Canyon entry is at N38 04.374 W109 43.596 which has some brush and small trees, blocking the view of the canyon. This face panel is found by hiking about 1200+ yards southwest into this canyon/wash as shown on the topographic map above. Look for a ruin to the upper left at N38 04.067 W109 44.100 just off the trail. To your right is a short trail 30-yards to the **panel** located at ground level. N38 04.100 W109 44.004. It is not visible from the canyon wash.

M 6.6 (est.) A large overhanging cliff prohibits high profile vehicles (over 2 yards) from passing. A nasty road boulder adds to the frustration. Just before this ledge is a small turn around area in deep sand. We suggest parking at **M 5.9** and walking.

M 6.8 (est.) **Castle Arch Trailhead.** N38 03.826 W109 43.898. It is a 100-yard walk to view this delicate arch, situated on a distant high butte.

It is approximately 200 feet wide and 150 feet high (61 m x 46 m). Its narrowest point is about 6 feet (1.8 m) thick. Distance to the arch is about 0.8 miles one way. Road now becomes rough.

9 Faces Pictographs Panel

Entry into another canyon is about 50 yards south of Castle Arch trailhead. Then east in another canyon. As you entry this canyon, try to walk up to the mesa and walk on the left side. It is approximately 150 yards to this south facing panel under a large ledge where it splits off the cliff wall. N38 03.772 W109 43.806. There are two panels. Video: https://youtu.be/7uB6ltJHblo

7.0 (Est.) Fortress Arch Trailhead. A 700-yard trail leads to a view of this large and sturdy arch on a high distant butte.

End of Tour

* *

Tour 1-03-05 - Beef Basin & Bobby's Hole

This remote area was once cattle grazing farm land due to abundant grass and a reliable water spring. Consequently, it attracted ancient Indians who left behind their ruins. One ruin is a spectacular well-preserved village-ruin. This road passes by Salt Creek hiking trailhead entry/exit.

Our last trip observed road deterioration at M 31.8. Due to the high elevation, there may (will) be snow/ice on the road at M 25, during the early spring and winter months.

If you have a <u>high</u> clearance 4-Wheel drive vehicle, you may be able to enter this tour from Elephant Hill in Tour 1-03-02 via Bobby's Hole. It depends on the extent of the last erosion. Verify road conditions at the Visitor Center.

Camping: This land is managed by the BLM and Forest Service having many branch roads for free camping opportunities.

Road to Beef Basin from Canyonlands-Needles Park

(Mileage is shown in both directions)

M 0.0/35 Exit at M 20.5 in Tour >> B to Beef Basin Road 107.

M 0.3/34.7 Pioneer storage house dug into a small cliff wall to the left.

M 2.8/32.2 End of improved road.

M 5.0/30 Start of sandy road for a few hundred yards. Safe high speed is your friend across sand.

M 9.4/25.6 Junction Road 180 to left.

Turn left to **Wilson Ranch** for 0.7-miles to a junction. Then turn right (Road 1041) for 0.5-miles to the Wilson Cabin/Ranch. All that remains is an abandoned cabin that appears to have been built in two different eras, judging from the log texture and colors. Abundant annual water from Cottonwood Creek is probably the reason for these ranch buildings being here. There are many large Cottonwood trees.

In order to preserve this historic location, do not touch or move anything. Supposedly, there is an Indian ruin in this area, but we could not find it.

M 17.5/17.5 **Big Pocket Overlook** - A narrow 2.5 mile (4 km) high clearance road ends at a peninsula that separates Salt Creek from Lavender Canyon. Consequently, it provides spectacular canyon views. Use binoculars to see Indian Village ruins and Kirk's Cabin in Salt Creek Canyon. Recommend driving to the end to understand the canyon twisted path that you will be hiking.

Cathedral Butte – Salt Creek Trailhead

M 17.7/17.3 Parking area for Salt Creek Canyon Trailhead. Elevation: 7,084 feet (2,159 m). N37 57.004 W109 42.295.

M 20.5/14.5 **Manti-La Sal National Forest** border and cattle guard. There is a 14-day camping limit sign. This is the western border of BLM land.

M 23.6/11.4 Sign: *Salt Creek Canyon view*. There is no parking area.

M 24.9/10.1 Cattle guard. Artificial reservoir to capture water for open range cattle. There may be ice on the road from here to M 25.

M 25.0/10 Approximate top of mountain at an elevation of 8,259-feet (2,517 m).

M 25.4/9.6 Junction: N37 54.351 W109 47.403. Sign:
>West (right) to Beef Basin (104) – 12-miles.
>Straight; to Gooseberry Guard Station - 5-miles and Kigalia GS – 19-miles (224).

Turn Right to Beef Basin
M 27.3/7.7 Another view of Salt Creek Canyon and Cathedral Butte east.
M 28.4/6.6 Sign: ***BLM Monticello District and Cattle guard. Eastern BLM border and western border of National Forest.***
M 31 to M 32, it is a 4-wheel drive road with sand on the road coupled with a hill.
M 32.1/2.9 Balancing rock on the south side of the road.
If driving east, a silhouette of an elephant is situated on the rim, on the west side of the balancing rock.

House Park Area and Ruins
M 33.8/1.2To the far left is an alcove at ground level. N37 58.401 W109 50.904. This is an unusual ruin because it does not face south to absorb the sun's rays. Consequently, it was probably a summer Indian farming home.

One remaining wall is separated from the adjoining wall, but it is supported by a log to prevent collapse.

Mel Turner's Cabin

M 33.9/1.1 A 0.7-mile narrow road left to Mel Turner's Cabin. The cabin is about 200 yards after the road ends at the base of a canyon. N37 58.054 W109 51.371.

This cabin was built sometime between 1885 and 1910. Verbal history recalls Mel was born in Maine on 19 February 1853 and moved here about 1880.

Eventually, he built a herd of 800 cattle. Apparently, he sold his property and cattle to one of the local large ranchers. Thereafter, he moved to Colorado, establishing a cattle ranch and tried uranium prospecting.

There are two distinct house sections. The first is a classical horizontal hand hewn pine log cabin using a special very wide blade axe to create a flat surface. Inside is a stove made by modifying a 50-gallon steel barrel. At the top is a wood entry door with holes in the middle for air and at the bottom to extract ashes.

The other house section was constructed of vertical small cedar logs, that have collapsed. At the end of this room is a stone fireplace, suggesting this was the living room.

M 34.6 Sign for Beef Basin.
At Beef Basin Loop
Maps: 7.5-minute topo maps are Fable Valley and Bowdie Canyon East. Bowdie shows a tiny western segment of Fable Valley Trail.

M 35.0/0.0 Junction at Beef Canyon Loop at an elevation of 6,500-feet (1,981 m). There is also a park sign-in box to record your entry. The purpose is to rescue YOU in the event of an accident. About 300-yards west on the ridge there are some ruin foundations at N37 58.830 W109 52.453.

1. Camping: The road to the far left ends at some shaded camping sites for one vehicle and one tent.
2. Stanley Springs - left (south) **on Road 104,** which is the **Loop Tour**. There are some ruins.
3. Right to Ruin Park – On Road 119 to Middle Park, Ruin Park and Pappy's Pasture.
4. Also, right to Canyonlands-Needles via Bobby's Hole.

Start of Beef Basin Loop Tour

This is an appropriate name as one can easily visualize hundreds to thousands of cattle grazing this fertile basin. Consider the logistics of moving these cattle herds to a railroad terminal at Thompson Springs, located 35 miles (56 km) north of Moab.

The ruins on this tour are along the road on ledges. Unlike those ruins deep in alcoves, their mortar has eroded, causing some to totally collapse. Exception is Village Ruin that is protected by a deep alcove.

M 0.0 Junction of Beef Basin and M 35 above. Turn left on Road 104.
M 0.6 Faint road left to House Park Butte.
M 1.4 Road 104, right. Continue straight.
M 1.8 **Stanley water spring** with cattle trough, a reliable source of water. While there may be no cattle at its source, filtering is recommended.

M 1.9 Junction. Route 199 south (left) to Calf Canyon and Village Cliff Ruin.
To Village Cliff Ruin
This is the finest ruin in the area. It is located high on a cliff rim in a deep alcove, having about eight (we did not enter) rooms. Original wooden posts still protrude from the walls. Its strategic location affords a panoramic view of the eastern mesa. That is, this is a prime view housing lot.

This is a 4-Wheel drive road, especially after about 1/2 mile, where long bed trucks may have problems crossing a narrow creek bed. At mile one there are two ruins to the left high on the cliff. The first appears to be a granary in a small alcove, where only a wall remains. N37 57.386 W109 51.952. A more interesting ruin is above it at the rim that resembles a clam shell. It appears to have been inhabited, but only one sturdy wall remains. N37 57.454 W109 51.952.

After mile 3 (4.8 km), the road rises to a very large scenic mesa. After about 300+ yards a spur road to the right ends at a parking lot. N37 56.768 W109 50.703.

The ruin is to the distant right.

From the parking lot, there is a <u>very faint</u> trail south, that loops right to the ruin on sandstone rock, climbing about 250-feet (76 m) up the cliff. Turn right and follow the rim contour. The ruin is located at N37 56.774 W109 50.915 at an elevation of 6,840-feet (2,085 m).

Continuing on Basin Loop Road
Mileage assumes you did **not** go to Village Ruin

M 2.4 Narrow road left. Road becomes sandy.

M 3.0 Crossing Creek Wash.

M 3.3 Junction of four roads intersecting here, clockwise:

   a. After about 100 yards south, the road ends at a highly eroded 5-room pueblo ruin foundation located on a cliff overlooking Ruin Canyon: N37 56.710 W109 54.078.

   b. After about 200 yards, it enters a corral. Open/shut gates to the road into **Ruin Canyon**. This becomes a 4-Wheel drive road and after approximately 600yards there is a well-preserved granary on the left, N37 56.690 W109 54.118. Time prohibited further travel, but there should be a ruin village after an estimated 3 miles (4.8 km).

a. The third road <u>continues</u> the Beef Basin loop route below.
b. This is the return from the loop road above.

Continuing on Third Road

M 3.5 **Ruin** is located to the right under a rock ledge about 25 yards from the road. It has a splendid view of the valley. N37 56.835 W109 54.298.

M 3.8 and 4.8 are camp sites.

M 6.2 Junction of three roads. After a few hundred yards, it ends at a camp site. The second road continues for one-half mile to another camp larger site. Continue to the right.

M 7.2 **Fable Valley.** Trailhead Fable Valley is a very scenic canyon with several ancient Indian ruins, pictographs and petroglyphs.

At this point of the loop road, we recommend turning back as there is nothing of significant interest further.

It lies in the Dark Wilderness Area, thereby retaining its pristine character.
USGS map: Fable Valley

Canyon has seasonal water and springs.

Hayduke Trail

It is also part of Hayduke Trail, named after a fictitious person in the book written by environmentalist Edward Abbey: *The Monkey Wrench Gang.*

It travels 800-miles (1,300 km) of rough backcountry trails starting at Zion National Park, to North Rim Grand Canyon including the dreaded Nankoweap Trail. Then north to Bryce, passing through Canyonlands-Needles (Fable Valley/Chesler Park) and ending at Arches National Park.
http://www.hayduketrail.org/Maps.html

Ruin on a high cliff near pictograph site.

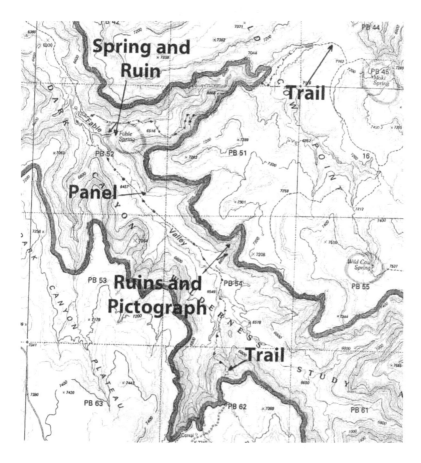

M 7.8 Road drops down into a narrow wash and back up. This should be Gypsum Canyon.

M 8.2 Road left into bushes. Continue to the right.

M 8.8 'Y' Junction. Turn right.

M 12.2 Major junction with a large corral. Turn right until you arrive at M 3.3 above.

To Needles National Park and Indian Ruins

From entry to Beef Basin at M 35, turn right onto Road 119 that ends at Bobby's Hole.

Middle Park

M 0.0 Driving north on Road 119.

M 1.5 **Granary Ruins** - Turn right (north) 0.8 miles on a narrow dirt road and drive to the end of the road.

A short walk towards the cliff leads to exceptionally well-preserved granaries. N 38 00.411 W109 51.284. Do not touch or enter!

M 1.51 Turn right (north) on a narrow dirt road. At about 0.5 miles, there is a large sunken water storage tank to the right for capturing rain/snow water that drains off the roof into the tank. After another 0.5-miles, the main road ends at a parking lot – very deep sand. N38 00.379 W109 51.722.

Note: Mileage below assumes that you <u>did not</u> enter either of the two roads above.

Ruin Park

M 2.9 **Tower Ruins** can be seen from the road N38 00.280 W109 53.863. This appears to be a two-story dwelling, as evidenced by a log embedded in an interior wall that supported the upper floor. The tower was probably occupied during 12201280 A.D.

M 3.2 **Junction** with Road 1111. Continue to the right on Road 119 to Bobby's Hole.

M 3.7 **Farm House Ruin**. Turn west (left). After about 400 yards, there is a stone ruin structure in the meadow. Continue on this road another 100 yards to a junction and turn right 400 yards to Farm House Ruin; the largest site here and park there. N38 00.539 W109 55.002. We continued down the road another mile, but did not find any ruins.

Walk up to the ruins. Some of this ruin was built underground as evidenced by the circular hole, typical of a religious kiva. N 38 00.279 W 109 54.915.

This village was a farming community growing corn, beans and squash.

At the junction above, turn left down the valley about 800 yards to another set of ruins. The tall ruin appears to have two stories. Of interest is the circular outer wall as seen at Hovenweep Ruins. Also, next to it, are exposed foundation also in a circular pattern. This was probably a religious kiva during partially into the ground.

M 3.8 Sign for **Beef Basin** when driving in the opposite direction.
M 4.8 **Entering Pappy's Pasture.**
M 6.4 This is the last camp site. Room for three vehicles.
M 7.0 End of road at a small parking lot. N38 02.050 W 109 56.365.

To Bobby's Hole and Needles Park

M 0.0 This is the normal exit from Elephant Hill, primarily to avoid returning up Elephant Hill. Once, this road had a firm dirt base and small rocks obstructing progress. After massive erosion, it is now a 4-Wheel drive road especially driving up the hill. In 2017, most the boulders were removed. That left loose and thick dirt that is a major challenge for motorcycles. Confirm road status at the Visitor Center if it is open.

From parking lot above, it is a moderately steep descent into Bobby's Hole. Unlike Elephant Hill, it has no sharp turns. There are a few other minor 4-WD obstacles past Bobby.

M 1.4 Old cowboy horse corral excellent for camping.
M 2.5 Park border gate (not locked). See Tour 1-03-02, Elephant Hill to continue.

* *

Tour 1-03-06 - Davis and Lavender Canyons

The road to Needles border is on BLM land, negating a permit. Camping is allowed anywhere. Camping is not allowed in the Needles park zone without a permit. Both canyons have many ancient Indian ruins and art; however, Lavender has more ruins than Davis. Davis has far more pictographs and petroglyphs.

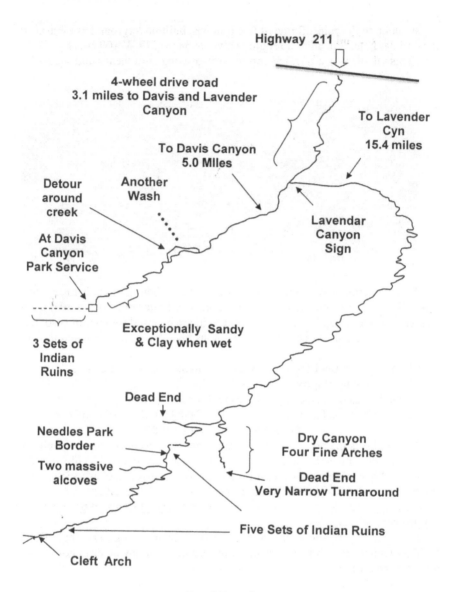

Road Junction

M 0.0 The route to both canyons starts at M 20.5 of the road to Needles Park. There is a large parking lot here on BLM land. The first 1.9 miles (3 km) are very annoying.

M 0.2 – Road straight – keep right.
M 2.8 Junction. Road to the right. Turn left.

Common Junction

M 3.0 Continue straight (right) to Davis Canyon or left to Lavender Canyon.

To Davis Canyon

Davis Canyon was probably named after Joseph Hames Davis, the original owner of the Donnelly Ranch along Indian Creek in the 1880s.

M 0.0 From common junction above, continue straight to Davis Canyon.

M 0.2 On a flat plane, there is a Y junction. Turn left.

M 1.1 Road left. Keep right.

M 3.1 (approximate) To the west there should be some ruins that we have nit explored. This community used water from 8-Mile spring below.

M 3.8 Climbed out of wash/creek and now under Cottonwood trees on a very narrow and sandy road with many turns. This is 8-Mile spring that once may have been very productive. There are no ruins in this area.

M 4.5 **Note:** There is a narrow road right. After a couple hundred yards, it ends at a dry fall with a small granary ruin above. The route to the ruin is by walking east about 125 yards where you can climb up to a ledge. Canyonland's border is straight ahead. This is a very serene campsite.

M 5.0 At the end of the road that is also Needles Park boundary. N38 03.994 W109 40.914. Park here and register.

As you pass through the fence, you are in Needles Park. Walk to the right side of this canyon.

5 Hands Ruin

Within 250-yards is an Anasazi ruin to the right. Inside the alcove, to the left, are five white hands on the wall. About 50-yards to right of the ruin, high on the cliff wall is a concentric circle petroglyph with a vertical line. There are two other faint petroglyphs adjacent to it.

5 Faces Pictograph

This is the prized pictograph of this canyon. This is a very well-preserved pictograph with 5 faces hidden in a small canyon.

About 600 yards from the parking lot, the canyon has a wide contour to the right where there is a small canyon. This is where the 5 faces Pictograph panel is located. It can be seen from within that canyon at N38 03.931 W109 41.213. It appears that this rock face was smoothed with a grinding stone before the paintings were made.

Video:  https://youtu.be/Re3bbA_LLlw

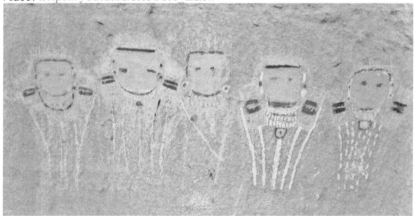

On the ledge directly under the 5 Faces Pictograph there are ten large depressions in the sandstone boulders, where Indian women ground their corn into flour. The depression is named *metate*, while the associated grinding rock is named *mano*.

Why did they carry their corn up to this precarious ledge to grind? I can't imagine a more uncomfortable place to sit and mill corn than this narrow rocky ledge under the pictograph. There can be only one explanation and that is the texture of this stone. It is amazingly smooth, relative to other rocks in the area. Therefore, these stones created the finest flour powder from corn or any other grains. One problem of using stone to grind grain is that stone grit in the flour quickly erodes teeth.

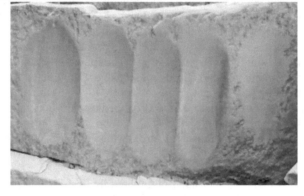

Canyon Hike

There are two canyon entries: southeast and southwest. This hike enters the large southwest canyon that is directly south of 5 faces. There is another smaller canyon to the right – wrong one. To ensure proper entry, we suggest walking south from the parking lot to the large far left canyon. When there, do not enter, but turn right hiking along the large wash that enters the second canyon where this tour begins. The GPS at the head of this canyon is N38 03.797 W109 41.278. After about 800 yards the canyon splits. Turn into the right canyon.

White Hands Ruin

At approximately one mile, a canyon enters from the right having an elephant head image at its entry, as shown below. N38 03.142 W109 41.951

About 200 yards into the canyon, there are impressive ruins on the north cliff we named *White Hands*. N38 03.187 W109 42.051.

These ruins are located about 30 yards above a sheer cliff wall. Consequently, entry to these ruins is impossible without a ladder or rope which is illegal. There are three sets of ruins best seen with 10X binoculars.

To the far right is a stack of logs that may have been a religious kiva as shown in the photograph below. Above them are a series of over 15 white hands and a series of dots under them. A larger image shows a box with a large hand over it.

We hiked another 800 yards into the canyon and did not see any more ruins.

Y-Junction

At about 400 yards further, there is a Y junction having this unique very high butte seen below. N38 02.917 W109 42.345. It is about 1,200 yards to the end of the canyon to the right.

The back half is a mini-Zion canyon with sheer vertical wall. About 200 yards before the end is an impressive alcove, but no indication of any inhabitants. We did not hike into the left canyon.

To Lavender Canyon

David Lavender was a local rancher and a book author of that era titled: *One Man's West* that is basically his autobiography. He purchased cattle from Al Scorup. He was described as a romantic cowboy wearing a colorful bandana and unique riding pants. That is: a *dude*.

M 0.0 At **Common Road** Junction, mile 3.0 above, turn left to Lavender Canyon, where water on the road is common.

A <u>backcountry permit</u> from the Visitor Center is required to open a gate at mile
11.7 below.

M 1.5 "Y" Junction. Turn right through gate.

M 9.7 In canyon.

M 9.9 Junction to Dry Fork Canyon to the left N38 01.645 W109 39.141.

* *

Short Tour to Dry Fork Canyon

This canyon has a few arches with the first being the best.

M 0.0 Narrow Road 1297, to the left, enters a canyon that ends at a small turnaround after 1.6-miles (2.6 km). The last 1/4 mile requires a 4-Wheel drive vehicle.

M 0.2 The first **arch** is to the right. It also hosts an attractive alcove. Walk inside and look up for the arch partition.

M 0.8 Here is a 20-foot (6 m) high double arch at ground level. N38 01.151 W109 39.42 at the road.

M 1.0 "Y" Junction. Turn left and see a **large arch** on the left that is more an alcove with a hole created by erosion from the top, rather than the side. Thus, it is a pothole arch.

M 1.5 A very sharp 100-degree turn downhill and steep uphill, that should be avoided by pickup trucks.

M 1.6 A large parking area. N38 00.725 W109 39.116.

M 1.8 End of road. A faint cow trail leads to the canyon.
****

This is a continuation of above, assuming **you did NOT** enter Dry Fork Canyon.

M 10.5 Canyon **Junction to the right;** (N38 01.519 W109 39.643). Visible only on return trip. Do not enter as it ends after 0.9 miles.

5 Granary Ruin

M 10.9 A narrow road to the right. N38 01.350 W109 39.565 at the road. Drive down this canyon about 300-yards to well-preserved granary (assumption) ruins that are not accessible from the ground level. Never have we seen this many storage structures clustered together with perhaps the exception of Nankoweep Ruins at the North Rim of the Grand Canyon (Book 3). It also appears that a home was here by the size of the rubble pile.

NOTE: When returning past this junction, the main road takes a long curve to the right. Just after the start of that turn, there is a narrow dirt road directly ahead. See M 10.5 above.

Park Boundary—Locked Gate

M 11.7 Park Boundary with gate, where you need a permit and lock combination to enter. N38 01.064 W109 39.057.

M 12.2 Road to the right is West Fork Lavender Canyon. N38 00.590 W109 39.885. This is where the **Long (thin) Arch** is located. Climbing up to the base of that arch is a mountain climber's task.

The road ends at about 2.5 miles (4 km). Estimated location: N38 00.255 W109 41.590.

M 12.9 Small **ruins** in a low alcove to the right, hidden by rubble. N38 00.266 W109 40.136.

M 13.0 Cylindrical **ruins** in mid-alcove to the left. N38 00.248 W109 40.178.

M 14.1 Look back to the left for a superbly preserved **ruin,** with its log-pole roof still intact. N37 59.647 W109 40.615.

M 14.4 Look back to the left for **ruins.** N37 59.489 W109 40.763.

M 14.8 **No-name Arch** high on the cliff to the left/straight. N37 59.385 W109 40.968.

M 15.4 Huge alcove to the right. M 15.6 **Cleft Arch.** N37 59.014 W109 41.630. Better views are further down the road.

Under **Cleft Arch** is a parking area by trees. N37 59.101 W109 41.521.

Cleft Ruins

Stop under a large tree adjacent to this arch. There is a very well-preserved 3-room family ruin, hidden in a small alcove above a very narrow canyon. It cannot be seen from the road or from the bottom of the arch (these are not in the arch itself).

However, from the ruins there is an excellent canyon view.

Access is only by a rock/boulder <u>crawling</u> south of the <u>base</u> of the cliff below the arch and then up to an alcove. Scrambling skills and long fingernails are required. They can be viewed from across the narrow canyon. N37 59.105 W109 41.609.

M 15.7 "Y" junction. Road left has the better canyon scenery. The road is very narrow with annoying rocks ending at M 15.9. A 600-yard hike ends where a 30yard (or so) loop arch is clinging onto a large slickrock base to the right. It is a scenic canyon with a dry waterfall to the left. N37 58.592 W109 41.908.

Appendix 1 - Dugout Ranch History

The general area from Indian Creek to Cottonwood Creek was always attractive to pioneers dating back to 1885. In 1895, Dave Goudelock established a credible ranch in Cottonwood Creek area described in Tour 1-03-05 in Beef Basin.

Al & Jim Scorup History

The real story is that of rancher Al Scorup and his Dugout Ranch. Al was born in 1872 into this poor farm family raising sheep and cows. As a boy, his sheep herd grew to 400, at which time he immediately traded them for cattle. By his early teens, he was herding up to 1,500 cattle and working cattle in Omaha, Nebraska.

In 1891, at age 19, Al was hired by Claude Sanford to find and manage a herd of about 150 cattle wandering in White Canyon, north of Natural Bridges National Monument. The process was to purchase cattle, let them roam having natural calves and then in the spring season, harvest the herd. Al would receive 30% of the surviving calves—not a good Las Vegas bet! Al knew his future was cattle so his mother made a couple of crude quilt blankets for him. With $5.00 in his pocket, he rode 300 miles (480 km), crossing the cold Colorado River at Dandy Crossing to find and herd those wandering cattle.

This was unsettled land – open range without borders except by gentleman's mutual agreements. Al's land was barren and lonely. Soon he was out of food and had to earn money. He corralled his herd in a canyon and got a job with Texas cattlemen driving cattle from Utah to Colorado. When he returned to his herd in White Canyon, Texas cowboys drove him out. Rather than be deterred, he went back to his home in Salina and obtained 300 more cattle and convinced his brother, Jim, to join him. After an enormous effort to move the cattle across the cold Colorado River, he herded his cattle on the rugged north side of White Canyon away from the hostile Texans. They were now confirmed cattlemen. They also herded the former 150 cattle into this area. Al was now twenty-years old. They lived in caves and built dams to capture precious water. They had to kill hundreds of wild horses to insure food for their cattle. They hunted lions and wolves that ate their calves. The first season was horrible; however, in the summer of 1893, Al and his brother Jim were able to brand (burn image into flesh) 300 calves.

That same summer, cattle ranchers from Bluff herded 1,300 cattle and 300 horses into White Canyon. It was a continual battle for food and water, but by spring Al won. The Bluff ranchers lost about 900 of their cattle and abandoned the canyon. Ironically, the Bluff ranchers were impressed by the Scorup brothers and offered Al a job for $37.50/month to herd the cattle back to Colorado. They needed the money so Jim stayed with the herd while Al took the job. This continued for a few years with Al returning to help Jim whenever possible.

In January of 1895, Al finally married his Bluff city sweetheart, Emma, at the Temple in Salt Lake City, Utah. Winter weather prohibited their return until the spring season; therefore, his brother Jim was forced to maintain the herds alone in these isolated and cold canyons. Al returned in the spring of 1895 to find a disheartened brother. Their herd was now down to 125 cattle, some of which were not theirs; yet Al convinced Jim to continue. Bad weather during 1896 and 1897 reduced their herd to forty-cows and only a few calves.

Al got a job with Bluff ranchers retrieving wild cows in remote rugged canyons at $5.00 per cow. By spring Al and his friends brought back over 2,000 cattle and that put $10,000 in their pockets! In 1898 they were able to purchase the failing Bluff rancher herd. In 1899, they purchased cattle from the Indian Creek Company and others. Their cattle ranching enterprise was growing.

By 1912, they had a recognized cattle brand known as the Lazy-T; hardly an apt description of their efforts. Over a thousand cattle grazed on land from the junction of the Colorado and San Juan Rivers to the Blue Mountains near Monticello.

By 1918, they were successful ranchers. Al had a home in Provo, Utah. They decided to sell their ranch to Jacob Adams and family for $252,700, including their property in Bluff. Thereafter, the Scorup brothers moved to Sevier County and purchased a smaller ranch for $90,000 where Loss Creek flows into the Sevier Valley. There, he herded sheep for his father. They continued to purchase purebred Hereford cattle to raise prime breeding bulls. Jim and Al could now live in houses instead of cowboy caves.

In late 1918, Al learned that David Goudlock was considering selling his Indian Creek Ranch that had a capacity for 7,500 cattle. Al, with brother Andrew and Will (Snuffy) Somerville, purchased it for $426,000 with a $50,000 down payment in cash, taking possession on 1 November. The new company also acquired Dark Canyon grazing area (near Hite Marina). Now, their cattle empire spanned 150miles (240 km) from the Colorado River to this area, greater than the size of Rhode Island.

On 9 November, the worst snow storm in Utah fell on the area, covering all grass lands with three-feet (0.9 m) of snow, burying cattle grasses while the winter continued. Al dedicated himself to preserving the herd. By spring, almost 2,000 cattle died and the rest were starving. He sold their hides for $0.28 a pound to gain some working money. No one expected Scorup to survive. He and his ranch workers agreed not to accept any wages for work to make the ranch survive. History records one worker receiving only 80-cents for the year of which 70-cents was spent for tobacco.

Now at the age of 50, Al was spending 16-hours each day herding cattle from one grazing area to the other while living in "cowboy caves".

Al and his men up to six weeks to gather the cattle and move them to Thompson (north of Moab) where they were loaded on the railroad. By 1921, cattle prices were increasing from $20.00 per head to $25.00 in 1923. On 26 October 1926, the ranch was further consolidated as the Scorup & Sommerville Corporation, with Al the major stock holder. Harve Williams from

Oklahoma joined in 1927 when the company had forest service permits to graze 6,780 cattle—the largest in the U.S. At its peak, the grazing area covered almost 2,000,000 acres (809,371 ha.) the largest ranch in the U.S. at the time. In 1928, Al sold 4,400 cattle for $194,000, allowing the remaining $100,000 of the Goudlock loan to be paid off. The ranch never had financial problems again, with 7,000 to 10,000 cattle grazing their lands.

Even at the age of 60, Al continued to herd cattle, but at a slower pace. Most of the work was done by his in-laws and nephews. He ran the ranch until he was 80years old, when a stroke crippled him and stopped him from riding a horse. Management passed to his son-in-law Harve Williams. Al's wife Emma died in 1935 and Al died on 5 October 1959 at the age of 87. He was inducted into the Cowboys Hall of Fame. It all started at the age of 19 by crossing the cold Colorado River, to take care of 150 cattle in a remote cold canyon for a 30% share of the calves, if any.

In November 1965, all rights were sold to the Charley Redd family of La Sal, Utah. The ranch name retains its historic name of Indian Creek Cattle Company.

Appendix 2 Desert Hiking Medical Problems

Obviously, most medical problems are incurred by those who walk trails that are beyond their physical capability. The first rule is to know all medical problems listed below. Second, always travel with a companion. The third rule is not to abandon a victim, hoping someone will come to assist. Of course, the latter has to be tempered with present hiking conditions.

Heat exhaustion is also known as heat prostration or heat collapse. The most common cause is dehydration after strenuous physical activity, causing excessive sweating in a hot desert environment, like hiking back up Grand Canyon in summer. That is, the body loses more water than it absorbs. **Caution**: read Hyponatremia below.

One can lose up to two-quarts (1.9 l) of liquid each hour in this hot environment. Thus, hot blood remains close to the skin surface to be cooled; however, there is less cool blood liquid recycling to cool your interior body. This results in further loss of large amounts of fluid and electrolytes in the body, including salt. Park Rangers treat up to 20 heat exhaustion cases each day at the Grand Canyon bottom.

Drinking a measured amount of water at 30- minute intervals (approximate) **is critical** as opposed to only drinking when you are thirsty. Waiting to drink is a huge mistake as thirst is not always an evident symptom.

Color of urine is a critical indication. The more yellow the color of your urine, the greater is the danger of dehydration.

Symptoms: **Any one symptom**, not all, is a concern. They can include: a pale face color, stomach cramps, weakness or actual fainting, vomiting, dizziness, headache, pupils dilated, clammy and moist skin, rapid shallow breathing and a rapid heart pulse. An extreme symptom can be muscle cramps. An elevated body temperature is NOT considered a symptom. Thus, the victim could have pale colored skin that could be cool and clammy to the touch, which is serious.

Treatment consists of moving the victim into a cool, shady place immediately. Elevate feet to allow blood flow into the head. Have the victim drink liquids with electrolytes (Gatorade, or equivalent). The victim must also eat food, especially high-energy food, to avoid a dangerous low salt condition. Remove restrictive clothing, fan cool air on the victim and slowly apply wet/damp towels. Don't throw the victim in a tub of ice. Because there is danger of cooling too quickly, the body responds by initiating shivering, resulting in increased body heat. If there is no major improvement, get medical help quickly. If all symptoms are not resolved within two hours, see a doctor. In any case, stop all physical exertion for at least a couple of days.

Heat cramps are muscle pains caused by excessive blood acid compounds and an excessive loss of fluids in the large muscle groups, generally the legs or arms. While not life threatening, they can be relieved by massaging the cramped muscle, taking short sips of water at 10 to 20-minute intervals (don't gulp) and keeping cool. Avoid liquids with alcohol or caffeine. If none of these help, medical attention should be considered.

Unlike heat exhaustion, **heat stroke** can occur very quickly. It is a life threatening problem, because the entire body's cooling system stops functioning. Heat Stroke is the next evolution of Heat Exhaustion and, therefore, very dangerous. At this stage, the body cannot cool itself. This is the most common heat illness in the canyon.

Symptoms include: hot body temperature over 104 degrees F (40 C) and confusion, loss of balance, disorientation, behavioral changes including seizures. Other symptoms are: feeling faint, red colored skin including axilla that is hot and dry to the touch. More symptoms may include: a fever, rapid and weak heartbeat, dilated eye pupils, deep breathing, followed by rapid shallow breathing, muscular twitching, confusion or hallucinations. Additional symptoms may be: a delirious or unconscious state of mind, talking incoherently coupled with a loss of balance while walking. It can quickly escalate to unconsciousness, seizures and possible death. In 1988, a Ranger in Grand Canyon found it unusual that a woman became comatose after she tried to eat her flashlight.

Treatment consists of getting professional emergency help **immediately as death** could be imminent.

Meanwhile, quickly find a cool, shady location and lay the patient down with the head level below the heart to bring blood back into the brain. Immediately cool the body, using all methods to quickly cool the body, except rubbing alcohol since it closes the skin's pores and prevents heat loss. This includes immersion in cold water, or lacking that, use constant wiping of the patient with cold water-soaked rags. If there is ice available, place it on either side of the neck, under the axilla and on the ankles, wherever there are large veins present to move the cool blood back into the central body. Loosen all tight clothing to allow perspiration to further cool the body.

If the victim stops breathing and has no pulse, administer CPR immediately. About 30-minutes later, when the victim is feeling better have them drink some water, take a little more salt and some food that will supply quick energy.

Magazines and other articles stress drinking large quantities of water, but fail to emphasize to also include salt and/or electrolytes. Thus, drink Gatorade (or similar) and eat salty foods (cracker or pretzels).

If the victim is unconscious, offer nothing through the mouth. A trip to the hospital should be the next action while keeping the patient cool (air conditioning, etc.). Start back to the camp immediately and see a doctor. There is no foolproof recovery--if you continue hiking, the symptoms may reoccur.

Hypothermia - Water Intoxication - Drinking excess water, while not eating compensating salty foods, results in low sodium/ion percentage in the blood, aggravated by losing salt through sweating. It is also known as water intoxication.

Symptoms are similar to heat exhaustion. That is: frequent urination, nausea, vomiting, and altered mental capacity. Treatment is for the victim to ingest salty foods immediately and rest. If mental alertness does not improve, rush patient to a medical facility.

Giardia Lamblia - Contaminated water could contain bacteria, named Giardia lamblia and/or another named Guardia duodenalis, which is also known as "beaver fever" or "backpackers disease". The only way to avoid this bacteria attack is to not drink polluted water.

Symptoms are: bloating, fatigue, flatulence (gas), abdominal bloating and cramps and fatigue. Additional symptoms are: weight loss due to diarrhea that causes the body not to absorb and digest nutrients. Symptoms vary between individuals. Those without symptoms become unknowing carriers of the diseases. After a maturation cycle inside the intestine, the trophozoite returns back to the cyst form and exits in your (or another animals) stool. A cyst is very durable and can survive at 37 F (3 C) for up to three months.

Bugs - The worst bugs are the *no see-ums* (slang for *no see them*) that suck your blood, leaving bumps on the skin that itch for weeks, especially around your head/ear area. We wear a baseball cap with fine mesh - finer mesh than required for mosquitoes - over your head and shoulders.

Horse and Deer Flies

Female Horse (big) and Deer flies (smaller) literally bite off a chunk of skin and suck your oozing blood so that they may reproduce. The adult horse fly can measure from 3/4 inch (20 mm) to one-inch (25 mm). They are found near wet areas. These pests attack in hordes much like Killer Bees. Their bites are very painful. The **only** protection is light colored body clothing with head netting. Repellents used for animals should not be used by humans, as it contains permethrin, which may be harmful to humans.

Note- While extremely rare, these flies can spread diseases such as anthrax, tularemia, anaplasmosis, hog cholera, equine infectious anemia and filariasis. Deer flies and horse flies are also suspected of transmitting Lyme disease. Allergic reactions may occur from their saliva, which is poured into the wound to prevent clotting, while the fly is feeding.

Bug Repellents

Mosquito repellent should have *Deet* as the active ingredient.

Cutter Advance Picaridin Insect Repellent is also effective against gnats (no-see-ums).

Lavender oil is a general natural repellent for pets and humans. A mixture of lavender oil, lemon and witch hazel can be applied to your pet. It is also a natural mosquito repellent.

A larger portable, mechanical/propane repellent for a 15 x 15-foot (4.6 x 4.6 m) camp area is made by Thermacell.

Made in United States
Troutdale, OR
02/24/2024